LONDON TRANSPORT COACH HIRES 1947-1949

David Ruddom & Ken Glazier

Capital Transport

First published 2002

ISBN 185414 259 3

Published by Capital Transport Publishing
38 Long Elmes, Harrow Weald, Middlesex

Printed by GS Graphics, Singapore

Front cover upper Blue Belle Motors Ltd was part of the United Service Transport group and this AEC Regal with a 1931 Essex registration stops in Grosvenor Gardens while journeying back to Norwood garage from which it is working on Route 2. The Duple body would appear to suggest that the coach has been rebodied at some date, probably mid to late nineteen thirties. The bus stop for the 2 and the 36 has been arranged for separate queues and passengers are waiting for a 36.   J. F. Higham

Front cover lower Bingley Brothers Ltd, who operated as Sceptre Coaches, owned two Bedford Duple OBs which, like Ivanhoe Coaches, they worked initially from Hammersmith garage and then in the first few months of 1949 from Putney Bridge. Smartly turned out complete with London Transport bullseye on the radiator, one of the pair, HYN700, waits for use on Route 14 through to Hornsey Rise. Clearly visible in this photograph are the distinctive round topped seats which Duple used on this model of coach.   Michael Rooum

Title page One is left to speculate what it was about this Bedford OB, framed by the Sutton garage entrance, that John Bennett of Croydon didn't like. Purchased new in July 1947, it was sold to J. B. McMaster and Son of Kingston-upon-Hull in January 1948. After nearly five years there it moved on to A. M. Parkin of Borrowash in Derbyshire and ended its days in the sixties with the Derby Rowing Club. During its brief stay with Mr Bennett, however, it performed on Route 213 in its livery of cream and brown.   Alan B. Cross

Facing page This atmospheric picture at Hyde Park Corner in a May 1949 rush hour shows Black & White Coaches of Walthamstow's number 22 helping out on Route 73. The vehicle started life as Green Line coach T 222 working from Watford in January 1931. It left London service in March 1939, initially to the dealership of Arlington Motor Company and found a new home in Wales with Starkey of Ton Pentre. It reached Black & White after the war and from this photograph it appears to have received a different body along the way. If on the other hand this is the original Ransomes built one then it has undergone some major surgery. Among the surrounding vehicles the delivery van of the Evening Standard with its roof mounted advertisement was a familiar sight along with those of the other two London evening papers of the time.   Alan B. Cross

Contents

Introduction

Between October 1947 and August 1949 London Transport hired, through the agency of the Passenger Vehicle Operator's Association, a large quantity of coaches which they operated as cover for 'no bus available' situations or as peak hour extras to help with the very heavy traffic demands of the time. The scheme is described in Ken Glazier's book *Routes to Recovery* and this book is an attempt to chronicle the companies and vehicles involved together with details of the routes on which the coaches operated.

Drivers were employees of the various coach companies and London Transport provided the conductors. Fuel was provided by London Transport and there were agreed schedules of mileage and route to be taken between the coach company's garage and the London Transport garage. Where necessary in the case of petrol coaches serving an all-diesel London Transport garage, this involved a detour to another London Transport garage to re-fuel.

Coaches first ran out on 23rd October 1947 and the last returned to their bases after duty on 19th August 1949. Between those dates the comings and goings were legion. One or two companies were listed on the original lists at the beginning of October but appear never to have actually participated. This may have been because their vehicles were not up to the standard or for some other reason. Some companies dropped out of the scheme during the summer months of 1948 in order to cater for their own peak hire period. There is even a letter on file from a company who only owned one coach asking to be excused for a week because they had failed to obtain a hired coach themselves to fulfil a long standing commitment. Others joined in the scheme at surprisingly late dates in 1949. As will be seen from a study of the list of coaches operated, several changed hands during the period and appear under two different owners. In total 945 vehicles have been traced as having taken part in the scheme at one time or another.

Operation of the coaches was fraught with problems as some of the correspondence files of the period have proved. Every coach was submitted to Chiswick Works for inspection and approval before it could be used. There is evidence that at times unapproved coaches were offered for service and on occasion accepted by hard pressed garage staff who failed to notice an asterisk on the list of vehicles provided from 55 Broadway. Such cases were picked up it seems in due course by sharp eyed accountants who were asked to pay for a coach that was not listed on their files.

Identification that the coach was operating on a London Transport bus service was initially provided by paper stickers reading 'L.P.T.B. RELIEF'. This was changed in January 1948 to stickers reading 'LONDON TRANSPORT' on two lines with small bullseyes at each end. However, in many cases these were not displayed and from August/September 1948 London Transport bullseyes were provided which could be fixed to radiators. A memo from the Chief Mechanical Engineer Road Services of 14th July 1948 reads 'Mr Burnell and I agree to the fitment of roundels as demonstrated to Mr Walker (of the P.V.O.A.) at Gillingham Street garage to all coaches. Arrangements being put in hand for production of 500 roundels and it is hoped fitment will begin towards the end of August'. Examples of these can be found in the illustrations. Basic route information was usually provided by means of paper bills fixed to bulkhead and side saloon windows. These normally gave the route number and the two extreme destinations being served by the coach. In some cases it was found that London Transport blinds would fit a coach's destination equipment and they were fitted.

A word of explanation is needed regarding the Country Area. The scheme did operate in parts of the Country Area but hardly any of the official documentation for this has survived. Such as has been seen is included but unfortunately there are likely to be considerable gaps in our knowledge of this area. In the Country Area there were subsequent schemes of hiring coaches for various reasons but this book is confined to the 1947 to 1949 scheme.

In the view of the authors, for the reasons touched on above, there will never be a totally definitive account of this scheme. This present volume originated as a project being undertaken by David Ruddom for the London Historical Research Group of the Omnibus Society following examination of the contemporary notebooks of Frank Mussett and Vic Walker. Surviving lists which London Transport produced, and a lot of the odd amendments and memos that have survived the fifty years which have elapsed, have been examined. In addition other contemporary notes have been made available, in particular by Laurie Akehurst, Brian Bunker, Alan Cross, John Gent, Derek Giles, John C. Gillham, John Marshall, M. J. Smith and Reg Westgate, who also gave access to the records of the late Ron Lunn. The work of contemporary photographers including the late J. F. Higham and D. W. K. Jones have been studied. Help has been forthcoming regarding the vehicles used from the records of the P.S.V. Circle and in particular Colin Bull, David Gray, Alan Mills and John A. S. Hambley. Finally Alan A. Townsin has provided some very helpful comments and added his own recollections of the period. Grateful thanks are due to all these and also to David Ruddom's wife, Enid, for calling over endless registration numbers in the search for accuracy.

It must be emphasised however that in studying all these records many discrepancies came to light. Typists' errors in compiling the endless lists of registrations at London Transport Headquarters were not uncommon and it was not unknown for contemporary observations to be mis-recorded. The authors have made their best efforts to establish the correct information but it is still possible that errors exist. In the final analysis however, as will be seen from a study of what follows, there may well be loose ends that can be tied up and possibly untold pieces of information which may yet come to light. It is hoped that publication of the listings in this book may encourage such revelations.

Recollections of the Hired Fleet

by Alan Townsin

When I moved to London at the beginning of 1948 my most direct journey home from work included a short walk between Charing Cross railway and Leicester Square tube stations to reach the Piccadilly Line. Yet substituting a bus ride was always a temptation, so I quite often diverted quite a bit from that simple course. As well as the attractions of the London Transport fleet, with anything from a 1930 ST-type to a glistening new RT, there was the fascinating collection of hired coaches. I made quite a number of journeys in them on various routes, occasionally in other parts of London.

The operators taking part in the scheme were independent concerns, from single proprietors with a solitary vehicle to sizeable companies, notably the Grey Green Coaches fleet of George Ewer & Co. Ltd of Stoke Newington, from whose fleet some 42 coaches, mostly Leyland Tiger, were registered for use on LT services. This figure represented about half the total in that fleet at the time, although the 42 coaches were probably never all in use simultaneously. Other substantial fleets came from United Service Transport Co. Ltd of Clapham and Valliant Direct Motor Coaches Ltd, of Ealing, with 27 and 26 respectively.

The vehicles hired fell into several categories. Many were almost new, the availability of coaches having resumed from the spring of 1946 after an almost complete absence of new vehicles in this class during the 1939–45 war period. Most coach operators were badly in need of such vehicles, not only for normal renewal of their fleets but because many had been depleted by wartime requisitions for military or civil defence use, such coaches often not returning or doing so in poor condition. The order books of the preferred chassis and body builders soon filled up, but the supply was augmented by firms less well known.

No doubt the inspection staff at Chiswick were very happy to pass almost new AEC Regal I or Leyland Tiger PS1 models, since such chassis had been chosen for T or TD class single-deck buses then newly added to LT's own fleet, and even though the coach bodies were less suited to bus work, they were too new to have significant failings. The Regal I was the name given to the early post-war model with 7.7-litre engine, which was in most respects similar to the standard Regal as being built just before the war – briefly the post-war version had been called Regal II until someone remembered the quite different pre-war model of that name. There were also a few of the Regal III model, at that stage almost all of the version with 9.6-litre engine, preselective gearbox and air brakes, so mechanically an equivalent of the RT double-decker.

Left This posed publicity photograph has at least two obvious anomalies. Firstly A&W Coaches vehicles never worked Route 159 and secondly the route bills were fixed behind the glass when the coaches were in service, not on the outside. Popperfoto

At that date, Duple was the most popular coach bodybuilder, in those days based at Hendon and hence particularly strongly favoured in the London area, and the post-war A-type curved-waist style was to be found on many of the hired coaches on these and other chassis. Harrington, based at Hove, was also very popular, considerably more so at that date than Plaxton, then barely started on its climb to becoming the largest of British coach bodybuilders and, like Burlingham, in those days less common in London than in the north of England.

Other chassis makes were less familiar, but no less welcome if in good order Maudslay, though an old-established firm, was quite a rare make pre-war but the post-war Marathon II and III were to become quite popular for a time. The two models looked alike but the Marathon II had quite an exotic six-cylinder twin-camshaft petrol engine – the last heavy-duty petrol bus or coach model offered in Britain. I was keen to ride in one, so one night found one of the Classique Coaches examples on route 38 and stayed on it for a mile or two, hoping the driver might get into the highest fifth gear but traffic did not allow. Even so, it proved very smooth and quiet.

The Marathon III was doubtless far more economical as it had the same AEC 7.7-litre diesel engine as the Regal I model, complete with AEC crash gearbox, so sounded like a Regal. I recall boarding one in Trafalgar Square on a warm summer evening to find its sliding roof open and the radio playing, giving commuters a strangely holiday-like trip home. Dennis Lancet coaches had been a popular choice for independent operators since the early 1930s and the Lancet III had fallen into line with most other full-sized post-war coach models by adopting a six-cylinder diesel engine, in this case the Dennis O6, giving very refined running. Daimler was better known as a builder of double-deckers largely for municipal fleets, though the wartime examples for London Transport were then still a familiar sight, but the CVD6 was beginning to catch on as a coach chassis. Lewis Cronshaw Ltd, of Hendon (though having origins in Blackburn, so its coaches were registered in that Lancashire town) put four on to LT hire work – they too were quiet and smooth-running and the preselective gearboxes made them better-suited to city bus work than most models.

Crossley was a much more unfamiliar make in London, best known then as maker of most of Manchester's buses, but was also beginning to sell its post-war SD42 model, with its own HOE7 diesel engine, as a coach; Viney's of Tottenham was one of those receiving one in time to put it into the London hire scheme. Tilling-Stevens had also resumed production with its post-war K6LA7 coach having a Gardner 6LW engine. Wiggs & Son, of Peckham, remained faithful to this make for its Grey Coaches fleet, including one K6LA7 as well as eight older models, including two of the classic Express B10A2 four-cylinder petrol bus type of 1930 originally owned by the West Yorkshire Road Car Co. Ltd. Dix Coaches, of Dagenham, had two new Guy Arab III coaches with chassis design much as the wartime utility double-deckers of that make but neater front-end styling.

Far more popular than any of these was the Bedford OB, the post-war model that was being added to coach operators' fleets all over the country and forming part of many of the hired fleets. As a vehicle to use on London bus routes, it was hardly ideal, with its bonneted layout, the entrance slightly set back from the front, the standard Duple body, called the Vista, usually seating 29 passengers. Indeed, some, including 14 out of the 15 from the Orange Luxury Coaches fleet of Keith & Boyle Ltd, had the 27-seat option.

The full order books of the main bodybuilders caused many hitherto unfamiliar names to appear among coach bodybuilders, some to prove short-lived. Quite a high proportion of the new Maudslay coaches had bodies by Whitson, a West Drayton firm, and other names included Dutfield, King & Taylor and some quite strange-sounding firms such as Yorkshire Yachtbuilders, this last having secured a contract to build coach bodies on the Daimler CVD6 chassis. Then there were older-established names such as Beadle, Strachans and Thurgood, all represented among new and older hired vehicles.

Less numerous than the modern coaches but at least as interesting were the older vehicles. There were a few of the wartime utility Bedford OWB, cramped as well as austere if they retained the original wooden seats for 32 passengers, although sharing the smooth and lively petrol engine, albeit with noisy gearbox, as found in the OB.

There were also a few forward-control vehicles which had been rebodied to utility standard. Perhaps the most interesting of these was a Daimler CH6, registered in Edinburgh as FS 6008, evidently a demonstrator but in fact first sold in 1932 to Redline Continental Motorways Ltd of North Kensington. This company still retained it though it had been rebodied in wartime by Burlingham, the main utility rebodier of single-deckers under the wartime arrangements, presumably for some contract work. It retained its sleeve-valve petrol engine and preselective gearbox, running well when I boarded it for a trip to Piccadilly Circus, though I recall noticing the usual slight blue exhaust smoke trail emitted by these engines as it drove away up Regent Street, the last sleeve-valve bus in which I rode.

The later pre-war vehicles taking part in the hiring scheme varied consider-ably in character. Some had changed hands several times, possibly with periods of military use, and looking well past their best. Others were still being maintained to very high standards, and had I had power to award a prize in relation to the coaches in which I travelled, it would have gone to Henry Saloon Coaches Ltd of Tottenham for HMX 175, a 1938 Leyland Tiger TS8 with Duple body to a rather restrained style in a grey/blue livery. It looked almost as new and ran superbly, its six-cylinder petrol engine so quiet when idling that it seemed to have stopped, and beautifully smooth on the move. The same operator also had an earlier Tiger on the similar-looking TS6 chassis, TH 3580, equally refined, but this had a new Duple coach body.

At that period, there were few second-hand buses from major fleets dating from later than the early 1930s yet on the market, the exceptions usually being oddities sold off as non-standard or which had not proved very satisfactory. More successful than might have been expected were some 1936 Leyland Cheetah buses with Alexander bus bodies from the SMT and Western SMT fleets; they were full-fronted and of quite striking if angular appearance. The

Scottish companies had specified diesel engines in line with their policy, firmly established by that date, but the 4.7-litre 'light six' in diesel form proved not up to Leyland's usual standards of reliability, which was doubtless why they were sold off much earlier than Tigers and Regals in these fleets. However, Smith's Luxury Coaches of Reading put some thirteen into the London hire scheme and they had been fitted with the petrol version of the same engine, which was much more reliable as well as sweeter-running – they were also smartly repainted in Smith's blue and orange livery and I recall a couple of agreeable trips on service 9 or 11 along the Strand and in the former case up to Piccadilly Circus in one instant with the sliding roof open.

Also in the oddity class were two Albion Valkyrie six-wheelers from batches originally placed in service by Young's Bus Service Ltd of Paisley in 1937–38. Although nominally buses, their Cowieson 39-seat bodies were of coach-like appearance and they were quite imposing vehicles. They were basically of type PR145 but in typical Albion fashion, the full designation had an 'SP' prefix, indicating special features. As built, they had Albion six-cylinder oil engines but my recollection was that one at least had received a Gardner 5LW engine – they were XS 4407 of Avonley of Deptford and XS 4765 of Ansell's of Peckham.

There were quite a number of former Green Line T-class AEC Regal coaches that had been sold off by London Transport around 1937–38, some rebodied then or later for further use in independent coach fleets and thus in a sense 'back home'. They could be relied upon to perform well, whether still petrol or re-engined with 7.7-litre diesel engines, as found in some fleets.

A make much associated with London independent coach operators in its heyday was Gilford, and among the hired vehicles there were a few examples of the 168OT model which had also figured quite strongly in the Green Line fleet after the take-overs of the early London Transport era. However, the later Gilford Hera model of about 1934 was also represented, with several examples from the Alexander and Western SMT fleets, sold off by then and acquired by London independent operators. They were noteworthy in being fitted from new with Leyland six-cylinder petrol engines removed from buses which had been converted to diesel.

Early Leyland Tigers of the types TS1 to TS3 dating from 1928–31 came from several of the independents, many having started life with big operators such as Alexander or Ribble, some having been sold off pre-war and usually rebodied in the same manner as contemporary Regals. Many such vehicles were to have longer lives in such form than with their original operators.

The quirkiest and oldest-seeming vehicles inevitably caught the eye. Perhaps the outstanding case was that of Omnia Transporters Ltd, garaged in Bromley, from whom seven buses it had acquired from the Eastern Counties Omnibus Co. Ltd were accepted for use from the former Tilling Bromley and Catford garages. Appropriately, five were Tilling-Stevens models, four of which were Express B10A2 models, DX 8047/9/92 dating from 1929 and DC 8590 from 1930, which had started life with the Eastern Counties Road Car Co. Ltd, of Ipswich, passing in 1931 to ECOC, which was formed to amalgamate companies in that area. Although the latter firm rebodied many of its older vehicles, these retained their original bodies, one at least by Thomas Tilling. Another Express, but of type B9A, had a chassis dating from 1927, and thus was among the oldest buses then still in service anywhere in Britain. Registered YF 1906, it had begun life with Motor Coaches Ltd of London WC2 and had been acquired by ECRC in 1929. There were also two Leyland Lion PLSC3 models with chassis dating from 1928–29 first run by the Ortona Motor Co. Ltd of Cambridge, though these and the B9A had been rebodied by ECOC in 1934–35.

Looking almost equally old were four buses owned by Mountain Transport Services Ltd of Chelsea, RC 408–10 and 426. They were of the SOS make built by the Birmingham & Midland Motor Omnibus Co. Ltd, better known as Midland Red, in most cases for its own use. The IM4-type vehicles in question had been built for the Trent Motor Traction Co. Ltd, at the time one of the several companies in the control of the British Electric Traction Co. Ltd which received SOS vehicles. In fact they dated from mid-1932, and thus were contemporary with, say, London Transport's 'Bluebird' 60-seat LT-class double-deckers even though the quirky appearance might have suggested three years or so earlier. I recall taking one, working on route 11 for a ride along the Strand and, once inside the BMMO-designed body, built by Brush, was reminded that the 'IM' stood for 'Improved Madam', the 'Madam' relating to design changes intended to make SOS buses appeal to lady passengers, with comfortable seats. The four-cylinder petrol engine proved fairly lively, the overall experience a good deal more civilised than external looks suggested.

A handful of double-deckers was included in the scheme. Lansdowne Luxury Coaches Ltd provided four AEC Regents, the two earlier ones, roughly contemporary with the London ST, were from the Burnley, Colne & Nelson fleet and were noteworthy in having centre-entrance bodywork, one by Roe and one to virtually identical design by Brush. Two ex-Halifax buses dating from 1937–38 had 8.8-litre oil engines and Park Royal bodies. Safeway, of Walthamstow, supplied a 1933 Thornycroft Daring with Park Royal body that had come from the Southampton Corporation fleet.

One of the benefits of the hiring scheme to someone interested in buses was the opportunity given to sample rare models. I had never ridden in a six-cylinder petrol TSM, these initials being used as a marque name by what had been the Tilling-Stevens concern in the early 1930s before reverting to the old name again. It was KJ 1612, originally a demonstrator dating from 1931, another vehicle in the Mountain Transport fleet, that put that right for me in a run to Kings Cross, for it was a C60A7 model, very possibly the first of the type, with chassis number 9001. It proved much as I expected, more refined than the familiar four-cylinder models, but had come on to the market at a difficult time and sold only in small numbers.

Clearly the intentions behind the scheme were much more down to earth than keeping an inquisitive observer happy and the growing numbers of new buses and overhauls of older ones allowed London Transport to improve the quality of its services and to dispense with the hired coaches. The scheme had its limitations but it had helped relieve the situation, at least modestly.

Garage by Garage

Alperton garage (ON)

Coaches operated on routes: 18, 83, 187

Operator	Dates
Gilbert's Luxury Coaches	21st June 1948 to 22nd July 1949
Valliant Direct Motor Coaches Ltd	23rd October 1947 to 7th February 1949
Smith's Luxury Coaches	16th November 1948 to 7th February 1949
Wright Brothers (London) Ltd (Cumfilery Coaches)	23rd October 1947 to 19th August 1949

A line-up of coaches stands in the Alperton garage yard ready for the off in the forthcoming peak. From left to right a 1947 built Maudslay of Valliant Direct Motor Coaches Ltd of Ealing is labelled for the 187 route, a 1938 Leyland Tiger also of Valliant is ready for the 18 and a more venerable looking Dennis belonging to Gilbert's Luxury Coaches of Wealdstone waits for duty on the 83. The pre-1936 style of radiator is at odds with the Kent registration on this vehicle – JKN885 which dates from February 1947. In fact this was a re-registration to Gilbert's of Tunbridge Wells, an associated company. Michael Rooum

Although largely Leyland, the Valliant fleet included two Maudslays, both of which were hired to London Transport and worked from Alperton garage. This one, SML50, stands in the garage yard prepared to work on Route 83. Unusually, instead of the normal end to end route label it seems that part of a destination blind has been adapted for display in the front bulkhead window. Whether an alternative destination was on the other side is not known. The strange spelling of Valliant, with two Ls, is not a quirky gimmick but arises from the fact that the company was started way back in 1927 by G. R. and W. D. Valli. In later years it would merge with Lewis Cronshaw and Venture Transport to become Valliant-Cronshaw Ltd. Alan B. Cross

Athol Street garage (C)

Coaches operated on routes: 56, 108, 108A

Operator	Dates
Bradshaw's Super Coaches	October 1947 to 21st June 1948
Clarke's Luxury Coaches	3rd August 1948 to 19th August 1949
Eastern Belle Motor Coaches Ltd	13th September 1948 to 24th June 1949
Fallowfield & Britten Ltd	7th February 1949 to 27th May 1949
Grey Green Coaches	21st June 1948 to 27th May 1949
C. G. Lewis (Lewis's Safety Coaches)	18th May 1948 to 22nd July 1949
Merry's Luxury Coaches	13th September 1948 to 9th April 1949
Safeway Coaches	21st June 1948 to 24th June 1949

The bus stop between the northern portal of the Blackwall Tunnel and East India Dock Road was not the easiest at which to pull up correctly. The driver of this Crossley belonging to Clarke's Luxury Coaches of Canning Town has made his best stab at it in order to decant any passengers after his subterranean journey beneath the Thames. The coach is working a schedule on Route 108A between Rochester Way (Well Hall Road) and Poplar and is not venturing north on the section of route to Bromley-by-Bow. Crossleys were not that common a sight in the London area and in this July 1949 shot the coach is about seven months old. Note the 'modern' addition of a radio aerial to the driver's cab. Alan B. Cross

The 'piggy-back' lines of this Duple body on Leyland Tiger chassis are perhaps a little exotic for the duties it now finds itself performing. A trip round the Isle of Dogs on Route 56 in April 1949 was a very different proposition to the present day surroundings of the 'island'. Although this route was the only Athol Street service not to make a dive under the Thames through either Rotherhithe or Blackwall Tunnels, the coach would have had to do so on its run into service being provided by C. G. Lewis of Greenwich. Alan B. Cross

Barking garage (BK)

Coaches operated on routes: 23, 62, 87, 145, 175

Operator	Dates
Barking Coaches Ltd	18th May 1948 to 19th August 1949
Battens Coaches Ltd	October 1947 to 22nd July 1949
Broadway Coaches (J. Grange & Sons Ltd)	October 1947 to 19th August 1949
Clarke's Luxury Coaches	20th September 1948 to 27th May 1949
Dagenham Coach Services	11th January 1949 to 24th June 1949
Dix Luxury Coaches	18th May 1948 to 22nd July 1949
T. W. Halpin	October 1947 to by 13th October 1948
Ideal Safety Coaches	26th January 1948 to 4th February 1948 and 21st June 1948 to 8th April 1949
Lacey's (East Ham) Ltd	October 1947 to 27th May 1949
Leighton Coach Co. Ltd	23rd October 1947 to 13th October 1948
Parkside Coaches	21st June 1948 to 8th April 1949
Pathfinder Luxury Coaches	24th January 1949 to 24th June 1949
Thatched House Coaches	13th October 1948 to 14th December 1948
Usher's Saloon Coaches	October 1947 to 18th May 1948

In the characteristic surroundings of the Becontree Estate, a typical 'day out at the seaside' coach of the day in the form of a Bedford OB with Duple bodywork seating 29 plies its route on the 145 between the Royal Forest Hotel at Chingford and Dagenham. This example, which was previously owned by Lacey's who had also run it on hire to London Transport, is provided by Barking Coaches Ltd, one of the smaller operators to help out. Alan B. Cross

The only example of an AEC 'Q' type vehicle to be lent to London Transport in this exercise was ARR 829 which by 1949 was in the ownership of Broadway Coaches (J. Grange & Sons (Plaistow) Ltd). This was new to Bevan & Barker of Mansfield Woodhouse, Nottingham in 1934. They traded as 'Red Bus Service' but at that stage it did not possess the streamlined styling as seen here. The bodywork is by Cravens of Sheffield and doubtless the seats next to the driver were well sought after. Here it makes its way through Dagenham to Becontree Heath on the 175 on a 'short' from Ford Works. Alan B. Cross

Battersea garage (B)

Coaches operated on routes: 19, 22, 31

Operator	Dates
Argosy Super Coaches	18th May 1948 to 24th June 1949
L. C. Davis & Sons Ltd	21st June 1948 to 13th October 1948
Grey Coaches (Wiggs & Son Ltd)	21st June 1948 to 22nd July 1949
Orange Coaches (Keith & Boyle) Ltd	7th February 1949 to 22nd July 1949
United Service Transport Co. Ltd (inc. Blue Belle Motors Ltd; L. Adnams)	23rd October 1947 to 8th April 1949
W. Watkins	21st June 1948 to 8th April 1949

Although based in Staplehurst, Kent the firm of W. Watkins provided one coach for London Transport use, initially at Streatham and then at Battersea. It was garaged first at the Astoria Garage in Gracefield Gardens, Streatham and then by October 1948 it had moved to the more convenient premises of Messrs Thomas Kent in Westbridge Road, Battersea. This Leyland Titan started life in 1937 as a Cravens bodied double decker, No. 149, with Portsmouth Corporation but the top deck was wrecked by enemy action at Eastney on 10th March 1941. It then went to the Merchant Navy Gunnery School and surprisingly came to Watkins as the coach seen here in Piccadilly in February 1948. J. F. Higham

The fleet of orange liveried Bedford OB coaches operated by Messrs Keith and Boyle as 'Orange Luxury Coaches' were a familiar sight on coastal services and private hire contracts in London at the time. No fewer than thirteen were hired to London Transport under the scheme and is typical of them. It stands in Greenland Road at Camden Town, which was the rather restricted terminus at the time of Route 31 which for so many years plied between here and Chelsea. The coach is working from Battersea garage but the 'leaning back' STL pulled up tightly behind is probably part of Chalk Farm's contribution to the route. J. F. Higham

Bromley garage (TB)

Coaches operated on routes: 47, 126, 138

Operator	Dates
Bickley Coaches	21st June 1948 to 24th June 1949
Castle Coaches (C. C. Grundon)	October 1947 to 18th May 1948
Cliff's Saloon Coaches Ltd	October 1947 to 19th August 1949
Omnia Transporters Ltd	18th May 1948 to 22nd July 1949

Previous page top The enterprising staff of Bromley garage, or possibly of Cliff's Saloon Coaches of Eltham, have discovered a London Transport blind which will fit the destination box of this Bedford OB. Hence the route number can be displayed by a label and a meaningful display shown. The driver and conductor of this May 1947 registered coach are nowhere to be seen as it lays over at Shoreditch Church before making the long trek back through the City, Bermondsey, Deptford, Lewisham and Catford to reach 'Bromley L.T. Garage'. J. F. Higham

Previous page bottom Omnia Transporters Ltd of Forest Hill were one of several companies around London in the early post-war years who thrived on keeping somewhat venerable vehicles in service. This Tilling Stevens B10A2 started its life with United Automobile Services Ltd in their Norfolk area in 1929. In 1931 the Norfolk area was transferred to the newly formed Eastern Counties Omnibus Company and the bus continued with them until disposed of in 1947 to Bird's, the Stratford on Avon dealer. Bought by Omnia this Eastern Counties reject finds itself in May 1948 working a key London service, the 47 from Shoreditch to Bromley. Alan B. Cross

VE 306 is another ex-Eastern Counties bus working for Omnia Transporters Ltd of Forest Hill on Route 47 at the Shoreditch terminus. On this occasion a non-standard route number is displayed and details of destinations seem also to be lacking. This bus also dates from 1929 when it was new to Ortona Motor Company of Cambridge. Passing with the company to Eastern Counties, this Leyland Lion PLSC3 was fitted with a new Eastern Coachworks body seating 34 in 1935 and its smart appearance here belies its age. D. W. K. Jones

Camberwell garage (Q)

Coaches operated on routes: 35, 36, 40, 42, 59, 59A, 137

Operator	Dates
Ansell's Coaches (S. Ansell & Co.; New Karrymore Coaches)	21st June 1948 to 22nd July 1949
Charles W. Banfield	11th October 1947 to 7th February 1949
D & R Motor Company	21st June 1948 to 8th April 1949
Elms Longman Motor Services Ltd	21st June 1948 to 24th June 1949
Grey Coaches (Wiggs & Son Ltd)	October 1947 to 22nd July 1949
Robin & Rambler Coaches Ltd	7th February 1949 to 8th April 1949

A fortnight before their presence will no longer be required, two coaches are parked in Camberwell garage yard ready for work on the 40 and 137 routes. While that for route 40 is labelled for the complete route from Herne Hill to Wanstead, the 137 displays a bill for the regular short working to Streatham (Criffel Avenue), a point just short of Streatham Hill Station. Grey Coaches have provided a Tilling Stevens coach first registered in Kent in 1931 while Ansell's have also provided a petrol driven vehicle of the same vintage, in this case a Leyland Tiger TS4.   Alan B. Cross

On another occasion the Leyland Tiger belonging to S. Ansell & Co. has been parked in a different point in the Camberwell garage yard. To the right is another hired coach belonging to Robin & Rambler while to the left is 0961079 which was a post-war AEC Regent RT chassis fitted with a suitably modified Tilling ST body and which was used as a training unit at the time. Eventually the chassis was used to form RT 4761. F.W.Ivey

Wiggs & Sons, whose fleet name Grey Coaches described their livery, seemed to favour secondhand Tilling Stevens. This example was new to West Yorkshire Road Car as their 286 in 1930 and has bodywork by United. It arrived in the Wiggs fleet in October 1938. Labelled for the 59A (Addiscombe to West Hampstead) service, it carries a slipboard destination of Camberwell Green probably used on its run in at the end of the morning peak. D. W. K. Jones

Catford garage (TL)

Coaches operated on routes: 1, 36, 54, 75, 89, 94, 124, 160

Operator	Dates
Avonley Coaches	5th April 1948 to 8th April 1949
Castle Coaches (C. C. Grundon)	23rd October 1947 to 19th August 1949
Julius & Lockwood	October 1947 to 22nd July 1949
Margo's	Photographic evidence but not on any lists seen
Omnia Transporters Ltd	18th May 1948 to 8th April 1949
R. A. C. S. (Royal Arsenal Co-operative Society)	23rd October 1947 to by 18th May 1948 and 13th October 1948 to 27th May 1949
Sydenham Coaches	October 1947 to 22nd July 1949

Secondhand Albion coaches usually emanated from north of the border and this six-wheel PR 145 with its heavy looking Cowieson bodywork carries a 1938 Paisley registration gained when new with Youngs of that town. Avonley Coaches was based in Lewisham and so it was appropriate that Catford garage used this contribution on Route 1, working the section between Lewisham and Marylebone. A 'Bluebird' LT passes along Marylebone Road in the background while the crew hold a conference. The 'PRIVATE' blind display looks very like a London Transport one and so maybe the coach has come off service for some reason.   D. W. K. Jones

This 1931 West Ham registered AEC Regal belongs to Julius & Lockwood is under the railway bridge in Waterloo Road while working on Route 1 to Lewisham in its basically green livery. A London Transport blind neatly fits the destination box providing a useful display to intending passengers. This is not the first time that Julius & Lockwood have operated on stage carriage services in London. Between October 1923 and March 1928 they operated three buses, mainly on routes 11B, 21D and 36A. Their bus interests were sold to London Public but their coaching activities flourished, albeit usually with elderly vehicles as seen here. Eventually in 1953 the business was to pass to Charles W. Banfield Ltd but not before another twenty-one months of London bus operation. J. F. Higham

A few former London Transport vehicles returned to run on LT routes during the coach hire period. One of the more notable was TF1 which had really been the prototype underfloor engined coach in 1937. It had a modified Leyland Tiger chassis classed 'FEC', the engine being mounted horizontally under the floor near the offside front of the coach. The body was built by Leyland and originally had an almost all-glass cab but it was modified to a more conventional form in 1940. After storage between April 1943 and January 1946 it came to Castle Coaches via a Chelsea dealer, Henry Lane, and remained in use until July 1954. Usually employed on Route 1 it is seen here carrying out a turn on the 36. D. W. K. Jones

Scottish Motor Traction disposed of quite a number of these full fronted 1936 Leyland Cheetah coaches with Alexander bodies immediately after the Second World War and several found their way to London area operators and on to London Transport services during the coach-hire period. This example, now belonging to Castle Coaches of Lewisham, has turned short at Victoria and is laying over in Grosvenor Gardens on 21st July 1948 before returning to Hither Green. 'Duplicate' is displayed on the destination blind, which seems reasonable enough in the circumstances.   Alan B. Cross

There were some coach operators who made their new smart vehicles available to London Transport. Among them was the Royal Arsenal Co-operative Society of Woolwich who contributed no fewer than eight of their beautiful maroon liveried AEC Regal III coaches with Duple bodies. Their number 63 stands at Catford labelled for Route 54 while alongside a 1931 AEC with a rather later style of body is set up for Route 1. This coach belongs to Margo's but interestingly its fleet number 26 is carried in similar style to that on the RACS coach.

Chalk Farm garage (CF)

Coaches operated on routes: 3, 24, 68, 74

Operator	Dates
Camden Coaches Ltd	23rd October 1947 to 7th February 1949
W. Cowell	31st May 1948 to 13th October 1948
Lewis Cronshaw Ltd	October 1947 to by 18th May 1948 and
	7th February 1949 to 24th June 1949
P. Hearn	23rd October 1947 to 7th February 1949
Overland Lismore Coaches Ltd	22nd June 1948 to 24th June 1949
Radio Coaches	21st June 1948 to 7th February 1949

This 1934 Maudslay with a Northampton registration originated with Osborne of Kettering but now belongs to W. Cowell. It is standing on the cobbles of South End Green, Hampstead Heath. In the background an STL of similar vintage is the more normal vehicle to be found on the 24 route in 1948. On some of the London Transport lists this coach is quoted as a Leyland Tiger but this photograph provides conclusive evidence that it was in fact a Maudslay. The bodywork was quoted by one contemporary observer as being by 'Spite' but any detail of that firm has eluded the authors.   D. W. K. Jones

P. Hearn was a name associated with London bus and coach operation, which can be traced back to the days of horse buses and the early motors. In 1906 and 1907 nine motor buses were owned which worked mainly on the Finchley Road from an address in Grays Inn Road. Still a coach operator in 1947 and now working from a garage in Northdown Street, Kings Cross, the registered address of the company was still Grays Inn Road as it had been forty years previous. Hearn was another company to use the Scottish Motor Traction cast off Leyland Cheetahs and this one, WS8009, rests under the walls of Kings Cross Station in York Way while working on the bifurcation of Route 68 which served this point.   D. W. K. Jones

Facing page top   The former C1 was another ex-London Transport vehicle which found itself back in use in the capital, although Route 68 was certainly not its former stamping ground. In fact it appeared during the period of the hired coaches under two different owners and on a London Transport list of 13th October 1948 it is actually shown under both. Here it is working for Overland Lismore Coaches, who garaged at Malden Road, Kentish Town, and stands at Beulah Spa, Upper Norwood ready for the trip to Kings Cross.   D. W. K. Jones

Facing page bottom   The coaches hired by London Transport presented a wide kaleidoscope of chassis makes and bodies. Among the rather more unusual was this 34 seater Guy now owned by Radio Coaches of Luton in Bedfordshire. FA is a Burton-on-Trent registration and was one of those marks belonging to a small area which lasted it seemed into infinity. FA1 appeared in December 1903 and by the time 5849 was reached it was 1935. The final FA registration was issued in May 1950. Appropriately enough this Guy started life as Burton on Trent Corporation No. 3. Although a Luton company, Radio Coaches had two London garages, one of which was in Grays Inn Road which is just beyond the Kings Cross road junction forming the background to this picture.   D. W. K. Jones

Chelverton Road, Putney garage (AF)

Coaches operated on route: 37

Operator	Dates
Hall's Coaches (W. D. Hall Ltd)	23rd October 1947 to 8th April 1949
United Service Transport Co. Ltd (inc. Blue Belle Motors Ltd and L. Adnams)	13th October 1948 to 27th May 1949

Route 37 is the only one of Chelverton Road's routes on which hired coaches have been recorded and only two coaches appeared from W. D. Hall and one from United Service Transport. Hall's 1948-delivered Bedford OB with Duple body is seen plying the route in its very dignified livery. The scene is redolent of the period, with the coach carrying a good load of passengers and one mother appearing to remonstrate with two angelic looking children. United Dairies are offering 'Price Reductions' and despite the austerity the shop window is reasonably stocked. Note the sideways turned bus stop flag to avoid Edward Kingston's shop blind.
Michael Rooum

Clayhall garage (CL)

Coaches operated on routes: 8, 8A

Operator	Dates
Cream Coaches Ltd (W. Couch)	21st June 1948 to 27th May 1949
Empress Motors Ltd	21st June 1948 to 24th June 1949
A. Green & Sons	21st June 1948 to 24th June 1949
Grey Green Coaches	October 1947 to June 1948 and 13th October 1948 to 22nd July 1949
C. G. Lewis (Lewis Safety Coaches)	18th May 1948 to 21st June 1948
Popular Coaches Ltd (A. Jones)	21st June 1948 to 8th April 1949
Radio Coaches	18th May 1948 to 21st June 1948

New in August 1948 this Maudslay coach of A. Green & Sons of Walthamstow gets rather wet as it heads into the City from Holborn on Route 8. Clayhall made a very tentative start in using hired coaches with only Grey Green providing them in the early period. Green and Sons commenced in May 1948 along with the other three operators listed above. This coach is dressed correctly with the London Transport bullseye fixed to the radiator and the route number and ultimate destinations clearly displayed in the front bulkhead window.   J. F. Higham

All the coaches provided by A. Green & Sons were new vehicles and were always well turned out. This 33 seat AEC Regal III stands at the head of London Bridge Street before turning on to the stand outside the station to pick up for another journey to Old Ford on Route 8A. Metropolitan Police regulations would require the door to be kept in an open position, which rather spoils the effect of the streamlined coachwork on this Plaxton body
Alan B. Cross

The elderly lady sizes up the leap she must make to board this Bedford OB which has pulled up rather a long way from the kerb. A small London Transport notice is carried above the driver's windscreen and the Old Ford destination is clear enough as is the route number 8. The destination blind has been set to 'London', which is a better alternative to the 'Private' sometimes shown by some operators. Popular Coaches came from St Leonard's Road, Poplar and the arrangement of the fleet name is a clever recognition of this.
J. F. Higham

Cricklewood garage (W)

Coaches operated on routes: 2, 13, 16, 60

Operator	Dates
A & W Omnibus Company (A & W Coaches)	23rd October 1947 to 8th April 1949
Lewis Cronshaw Ltd	October 1947 to 7th February1949
Curtis & Hearn	23rd October 1947 to by 1st March 1948
Lucky Line Coaches Ltd	18th May 1948 to 8th April 1949
L. D. Surrell Ltd	21st June 1948 to 13th October 1948
Venture Transport (Hendon) Ltd	23rd October 1947 to 8th April 1949

A & W Coaches of Harrow was a company which gave its coaches names – usually 'Lady xx'. OMY583 – number 36 in their fleet – is called 'Lady Irene' and is one of the fourteen Maudslays that the company made available to London Transport. It (or rather she) stands in the Cricklewood garage yard ready for service on the 16 route. Presumably the last company duty performed was a trip to Clacton. One of Cricklewood's many STLs waits alongside for its next stint on Route 60.   D. W. K. Jones

This 1947 Maudslay coach laying over at Aldwych on Route 60, with the Aldwych tram station entrance visible above the nearside wing, presents an identity problem. The barely discernible owner's name above the cab is P. Crouch & Son, a firm from Guildford and indeed the registration is a Guildford, Surrey mark. However, the livery, fleet number and name 'Lady Dorothy' all suggest it belongs to A & W Coaches of Harrow. The destination blind tells us it is 'On Hire to Golden Arrow', which is not very helpful. This coach was in fact on loan to A & W from Crouch who appear to have been an associate company.   J. F. Higham

Croydon garage (TC)

Coaches operated on routes: 12, 59, 64, 68, 133, 197

Operator	Dates
Bourne & Balmer (Croydon) Ltd	October 1947 to 19th August 1949
Jewell's Coaches	23rd October 1947 to December 1947
Progress Coaches (Freemantle & Dobson)	October 1947 to 22nd July 1949
H. J. Sargent	18th May 1948 to 8th April 1949
Shirley Coaches (A. Bennett & Sons)	1st September 1948 to 13th October 1948

There were two separate companies called Progress Coaches which hired vehicles to London Transport under the scheme. This is the one which came from the Sanderstead company, which kept their vehicles In the Hamsey Green Garage in Limpsfield Road. This 1932 full fronted Tilling Stevens carries a Manchester registration and has a central entrance body seating 32 passengers. Despite its age it gave stalwart service lasting throughout the period of Progress Coaches' involvement. The shiny surround to the radiator glints as it waits at Finsbury Circus. J. F. Higham

Although the banner above the windscreens reads 'Sargents of East Grinstead', Mrs Janet Sargent housed the three Bedford OWB's used by London Transport at Central Garage (Croydon) Ltd behind the Croydon Town Hall. The wartime bodies mounted on the Bedford chassis were very neat and practical given the restrictions which applied in their construction, and close examination of this example shows that comfortable coach seats have now been fitted. The driver of fleet number 03 waits at South Croydon for the London Transport conductor allocated to him for the journey up to Liverpool Street. D. W. K. Jones

What exactly the passengers might observe between South Croydon and Liverpool Street on this Harrington bodied 'Observation Saloon Coach' belonging to Bourne & Balmer (Croydon) Ltd is open to speculation. New to the company in 1937 this Dennis Lancet carries a Croydon registration as befits this well known coach company and appears to have survived the war years in good condition apart from a few dents in the panelling. It waits at South Croydon for the trip into town. D. W. K. Jones

Dalston garage (D)

Coaches operated on routes: 9, 11, 47, 78, 208, 208A

Operator	Dates
Boughton's Coaches Ltd	23rd October 1947 to 22nd July 1949
Empress Motors Ltd	October 1947 to 27th May 1949
Fallowfield & Britten Ltd	18th May 1948 to 27th May 1949
Grey Green Coaches	October 1947 to 19th August 1949
Pearl & Gunn ('The Fairway')	23rd October 1947 to 8th April 1949
John Pritchard	October 1947 to 24th June 1949
Safeway Coaches	23rd October 1947 to 18th May 1948 and 21st June 1948 to 24th June 1949
Thorpe Coaches Ltd	November 1947 to 4th February 1948
Usher's Saloon Coaches	18th May 1948 to 24th June 1949

Pearl & Gunn might appear to have golfing interests by their fleet name of 'The Fairway' as displayed in a rather battered light box. However, the more prosaic reason was that their registered address was 8 The Fairway, Mill Hill, although this coach, which was their sole contribution to London Transport, was housed at the Fallowfield & Britten premises in Bethnal Green Road. Standing at the Shoreditch terminus of Route 78 this 1933 Albion has Duple rear-entrance coach bodywork of a bygone era together with a roof luggage compartment probably reached by a ladder on the rear.   D. W. K. Jones

Safeway Coaches provided this full fronted Albion for operation on 'prestige' Route 11 which is seen at the Charing Cross end of the Strand. This is presumably 1947 since 'LPTB Relief' is displayed in the blind box. The angle and height of the steering wheel is quite amazing by today's standards. It is also interesting to note that the coach only has one headlight, the position for the offside one being occupied by the fleet number. V.C.Jones

As well as the Pearl & Gunn vehicle, Fallowfield & Britten also provided coaches from their Bethnal Green Road garage to Route 78. They had a sizeable fleet of Bedford OBs with the standard Duple bodywork as exemplified by MMT877 at Shoreditch Church. The Fallowfield & Britten company had been formed in 1947 by the merger of Fallowfield & Knight Ltd and W. & J. Britten's Superb Coaches. Eventually in 1952 Fallowfield & Britten was purchased by its rival Grey Green but that was after the period dealt with in this book.   J. F. Higham

Usher's Saloon Coaches of Bow only hired out one vehicle to London Transport and it was this 32 seat Leyland Lion LT5A with Beadle body, here pulling away from the stop at St Clement Dane's church in the Strand. The coach was used by Barking garage from October 1947 until June 1948 and then transferred to Dalston where it worked on Route 11. The registration indicates that it originated in Middlesex between May and July 1934.   J. F. Higham

Seven Bedford OB coaches were among the 42 vehicles recorded as being hired from Grey Green Coaches including this example, HYP560, which is ready for service on the famous Route 11 from Liverpool Street to Shepherds Bush. No-one would have thought at the time that Grey Green would fifty years hence be an important operator in their own right of London bus routes, but their pale green and grey coaches were a familiar sight in the late forties, particularly in north and east London. Beside the private hire work, which was the main use of these Bedfords, long distance services were worked to the coast from their depots at Stamford Hill and Mile End. Michael Rooum

There is a problem of identity over this photograph of a Bedford OWB/Duple laying over on Route 9 outside Broad Street Station. The negative was catalogued by Mr Higham as being of Boughton's Coaches Ltd but the registration was not confirmed. Boughton's are recorded as operating at least six Bedfords, only one of which has a wartime registration – CAW885 which was new to T. Hoggins of Wrockwardine, Shropshire in November 1944 and went to Greenwood of Ramsey, Lincs in April 1947. The style of bodywork and a close examination suggests this is that vehicle. The half painted out fleet name seems to indicate that it has only recently been acquired by Boughtons and the style of lettering for 'I Coaches' is very reminiscent of Universal Coaches of Edmonton but that is guesswork.   J. F. Higham

Edgware garage (EW)

Coaches operated on route: 140

Operator	Dates
A & W Omnibus Co. Ltd (A & W Coaches)	18th May 1948 to 22nd July 1949
Curtis & Hearn	1st March 1948 to 24th June 1949
Ray (Edgware) Ltd	18th November 1947 to 22nd July 1949
L. Tonge	October 1947 and 21st June 1948 to July 1948
R. A. Tyler (Gold Star Coaches)	July 1948 to 24th June 1949

Most of the operators listed above only operated for relatively short periods from Edgware garage and the 140 route between Hayes and Mill Hill is the only firm record we have of operation. Ray (Edgware) Ltd, however, did work three of the standard Bedford OBs from November 1947 through to July 1949. Here one of the three, MMT879, stands, possibly in the Edgware garage approach road, wearing the light coloured livery of the company. D. W. K. Jones

Elmers End garage (ED)

Coaches operated on routes: 12, 194

Operator	Dates
John Bennett (Croydon) Ltd	October 1947 to 27th May 1949
L. C. Davis & Sons Ltd	23rd October 1947 to 19th August 1949
Woodside Coaches	23rd October 1947 to 22nd July 1949

John Bennett (Croydon) Ltd purchased eleven of these petrol engined Leyland TS4 coaches with Harrington bodies in 1932. This is fleet number 17 which was given a new Strachan coach body in 1949 and continued with Bennett until 1958. Working the Oxford Circus to South Croydon section of Route 12, the driver seeks some relief from the hot engine alongside him while the coach stands in the West End at the beginning of its long run south.   D. A. Ruddom collection

Enfield garage (E)

Coaches operated on routes: 102, 107, 107A, 135, 144A, 144B, 205, 242

Operator	Dates
Careford's Coaches	18th May 1948 to 8th April 1949
Champion Coaches	18th May 1948 to 19th August 1949
Grosvenor Coaches Ltd	October 1947 to 24th June 1949
N. J. & K. B. Kilsby	21st June 1948 to 13th October 1948
Knowlers Coaches Ltd	26th January 1948 to 8th April 1949
Lily Coaches	13th October 1948 to 27th May 1949
Modern Super Coaches	26th January 1948 to 18th May 1948 and 13th October 1948 to 27th May 1949
Superior Coaches Ltd	22nd June 1948 to 22nd July 1949

The activities of the eight operators listed as working from Enfield garage are rather different from other garages with a large number of companies. In the main these were spread around all the routes operated by the garage but at Enfield it seems that each company had a rather specific one or two routes that were their province. In the case of Grosvenor Coaches of Baker Street, Enfield their three coaches could only be found on the 144B and the 205. Bedford OWB LMT880 is working the former and driver and conductor, both smartly turned out, pose for the camera in what appears to be the middle of the road at Alexandra Park.   D. W. K. Jones

Mr C. A. Champion of Champion's Coaches, Chingford, provided four coaches during the period, which covered three duties at Enfield and Tottenham garages. Two of them were elderly Gilfords including PG9575. The work at Enfield garage did not commence until June 1948 and was restricted to Routes 107 and 135. In the shadows under the canopy the route labels for 135 can be made out as the Wycombe bodied coach simmers in the sunshine between peaks.   W. J. Haynes

Forest Gate garage (G)

Coaches operated on routes: 25B, 40

Operator	Dates
Clark's Red Coaches	21st June 1948 to 22nd July 1949
Clarke's Luxury Coaches	23rd October 1947 to 24th June 1949
J. J. & B. R. Downey (Escort Coaches)	21st June 1948 to 8th April 1949
Ferndale Coaches	23rd October 1947 to 22nd July 1949
A. Green & Sons	18th May 1948 to 21st June 1948
Grey Green Coaches	24th November 1947 to 18th May 1948
Lansdowne Luxury Coaches Ltd	3rd August 1948 to 22nd July 1949
Majestic Luxury Coaches Ltd	October 1947 to 21st June 1948 and 13th October 1948 to 8th April 1949
Merry's Luxury Coaches Ltd	24th November 1947 to February 1948 and 21st June 1948 to 13th October 1948
R. A. C. S. (Royal Arsenal Co-operative Society)	23rd October 1947 to 21st June 1948
Radio Coaches	18th May 1948 to 13th October 1948
Safeway Coaches	3rd August 1948 to 27th May 1948
Sunbeam (C. J. Worsley)	21st June 1948 to 24th June 1949

Among the vehicles operated by Sunbeam Coaches of Walthamstow were a pair of somewhat rare normal control AECs. This ponderous looking coach, which actually only seated 29, is wending its way around Grosvenor Gardens at Victoria being followed by an STL which was Forest Gate's standard bus at the time. It bears a 'Regal' badge on the radiator although the correct name for the forward control model was the 'Ranger'. Forest Gate was an all diesel garage in 1948 and since AWJ232 was petrol driven it had to be taken to Upton Park garage to refuel at night.   Michael Rooum

Beside the normal control AEC coaches, Sunbeam of Walthamstow also ran a forward control Leyland Cub on Route 25B. This 1933 vehicle with a Nottinghamshire registration only seated 26 and began its stint on the 25B during 1948. Having traversed Bond Street it now heads down Piccadilly at Green Park Station followed by RT 44 on the 14 from Putney Bridge. This RT is one of those still preserved today.
J. F. Higham

This Gilford Hera with Wycombe body was new to Western S. M. T. in 1934 and was withdrawn by them in 1938 passing through a dealer to E. H. Banks of Forest Gate and then later to Clark's Red Coaches of the same place. They submitted it to Chiswick Works for inspection as to its suitability on 26th October 1948. Passing the scrutiny of the London Transport engineers it was put to work from Forest Gate garage on Route 25B and it is seen in the sunshine of May 1949 at Victoria Station. Of interest in this picture is the woman conductor on the left, still in winter uniform, with cap at rakish angle and Bell Punch firmly fixed to her greatcoat.
Alan B. Cross

The very busy Route 25B between Victoria and Becontree Heath with peak hour extensions to Hornchurch was probably home to the largest number of hired coaches of any London route. Two head this line-up at Victoria Station with the inspector doubtless anxious to trace the Radio Coaches driver to move up his coach. If it was an LT bus he would probably do it himself but the coach operators were adamant in entering into the agreement that they would provide the driver so he is powerless to do anything to prevent a jam back out into Buckingham Palace Road. This 35 seat bus originated with Gellygaer U. D. C. in 1931 but looks to be nicely kept by Radio Coaches, who while being a Luton firm used garages at Walthamstow and Kings Cross.   J. F. Higham

Ferndale Coaches (Brooks & Palmer) had registered offices at Rancliffe Road, East Ham but garaged their vehicles at Albert Road, North Woolwich. This smart Duple bodied AEC Regal seating 33 was one of three coaches they provided on the 25B route and it is rapidly filling up with commuters under an inspector's supervision in this morning peak hour shot at Victoria. The white painted top of the bonnet must have been a source of irritation to the driver on a bright day.   D. W. K. Jones

The 25B was unique in the hired coaches scheme in having two operators who suppled double deck buses. At first London Transport would not countenance them but relented during 1948. Safeway Coaches (Hunt & West) of Walthamstow supplied this Thornycroft Daring dating from 1933. An extremely rare breed – only 41 were ever built – this example was one of a pair originally supplied to Southampton.   D. W. K. Jones

The second supplier of double deck buses to Route 25B was Lansdowne Luxury Coaches Ltd of Leytonstone who supplied some AEC Regent 661s, this one with a Roe centre entrance body. Just to add to passengers' confusion it had twin staircases running forward and back from the central entrance. One has visions of fare dodgers using these to advantage, but perhaps 1948 was a more law-abiding time. The bus originated with Burnley, Colne and Nelson Corporation in 1931.   D. W. K. Jones

Hackney garage (H)

Coaches operated on routes: 6, 22, 30

Operator	Dates
Ansell's Coaches (S. Ansell & Co.; New Karrymore Coaches).	23rd October 1947 to 21st June 1948
Dryer's Coaches Ltd	23rd October 1947 to 18th May 1948
Eastern Belle Motor Coaches Ltd	21st June 1948 to 13th October 1948
Emerald Coaches Ltd	23rd October 1947 to 27th May 1949
Empress Motors Ltd	October 1947 to 22nd July 1949
Grey Green Coaches	23rd October 1947 to 19th August 1949
C. G. Lewis (Lewis's Safety Coaches)	October 1947 to 18th May 1948
London Road Coaches	3rd August 1948 to 1st April 1949
Majestic Luxury Coaches Ltd	21st June 1948 to 24th June 1949

Daimler coaches always gave the appearance of being the aristocrats of the coaching world, as indeed they had good cause to be. SML475 wasn't even built when the hired coach scheme commenced but Emerald Coaches were happy to offer it for service, along with its sister SML474. Despite the gloom of Holborn Viaduct its fluted radiator surround shines brightly. Emerald Coaches came from Islington and their official address was the rather strange 1232½ Shepperton Road, N1.   J. F. Higham

Empress Motors of Cambridge Heath owned a pair of these rather unusual Morris Commercial Dictator coaches dating from 1938. One of them is caught at the Putney Common terminus of Route 22. The open doorway illustrates the unsuitability of most of the coaches for stage carriage work in London. Negotiating the steps could only be done singly and the height, particularly of the second one, must have been difficult for elderly passengers. Even today you only have to watch coaches unloading 'Over Sixties outings' at the seaside to appreciate this. In addition where was the conductor going to stand? However, the extra seats provided where otherwise there might have been none were worth the inconveniences. Michael Rooum

When the War Department took over the entire fleet of C. G. Lewis (Lewis's Safety Coaches) of Greenwich it became necessary for Mr Lewis to purchase some secondhand replacements. A mixture of Albions, Bedfords and Leylands was acquired including this 1935 three-axle Leyland Tiger TS7T with Leyland body which came from Central Scottish Motor Traction. Here it is working Route 30 in Old Brompton Road from Hackney garage, a duty which Lewis gave up by May 1948 thereafter concentrating on Athol Street and Old Kent Road. When Mr Lewis had finished with the coach in June 1949 it passed to P. Currie of Dartford and after January 1952 ended its days used as an office. Michael Rooum

Hammersmith garage (R)

Coaches operated on routes: 11, 17, 88

Operator	Dates
L. C. Davis & Sons Ltd	October 1947 to 18th May 1948
Empress Coaches (J. G. Green)	October 1947 to 18th May 1948
Ivanhoe Coaches	21st June 1948 to 7th February 1949
Mountain Transport Services Ltd	18th May 1948 for a short period only
Orange Coaches (Keith & Boyle) Ltd	23rd October 1947 to 13th October 1948
Robin & Rambler Coaches Ltd	18th May 1948 to 7th February 1949
Sceptre Coaches (Bingloy Brothers Ltd)	21st June 1948 to 7th February 1949
Smith's Luxury Coaches (A. E. Smith – South East Area)	9th August 1948 to 22nd July 1949
Valliant Direct Motor Coaches Ltd	23rd October 1947 to 18th May 1948 and 13th October 1948 to 24th June 1949

Although eight operators are recorded as working from Hammersmith garage, which in 1950 would be renamed Riverside, none worked for the whole period as shown by the inclusive dates above. Robin & Rambler Coaches did not appear until the summer of 1948 and then in 1949 transferred their allegiance to Camberwell garage. Four of their Bedford OBs are recorded as appearing on London Transport services including JXB321, which rather unusually carried a Whitson body, and is seen on Route 11 at Victoria.　J. F. Higham

Hanwell garage (HW)

Coaches operated on routes 92, 97, 105

Operator	Dates
Smith's Luxury Coaches (A. E. Smith)	12th July 1948 to 19th August 1949
United Service Transport Co. Ltd (inc. Blue Belle Motors Ltd; L. Adnams)	17th November 1947 to by February 1948
Venture Transport (Hendon) Ltd	19th May 1948 to 13th October 1948
Wright Brothers (London) Ltd (Cumfilery Coaches)	October 1947 to 22nd July 1949

Also seen in the Alperton garage section of this book, Valliant Direct's Maudslay SML50 in the early days of coach hire in 1947 worked out of Hanwell garage, which after 1950 was renamed Southall. It heads west from Ealing Broadway on Route 97 to Brentford, which route was translated twenty one years later to become E2 in the Ealing satellite scheme. Alan B. Cross

An identical Maudslay coach to that operated by Valliant Direct from Hanwell garage in 1947 was worked by Wright Brothers (London) Ltd of Hanwell who were in fact a subsidiary of Valliant. The coach is waiting outside Hanwell garage (later called Southall) presumably to pick up the conductor for its duty on Route 105 from Southall to Shepherds Bush. The coach is well wrapped up against the winter cold. Note the traffic free Uxbridge Road. Alan B. Cross

Harrow Weald garage (HD)

Coaches operated on routes: 114, 140, 158, 230

Operator	Dates
A & W Omnibus Co. Ltd (A & W Coaches)	October 1947 to 22nd July 1949
Enterprise Coaches	18th May 1948 to 27th May 1949
Lucky Line Coaches Ltd	18th May 1948 to 27th May 1949
Parker's Coaches	18th May 1948 to 21st June 1948

No photographs have been traced showing Harrow Weald operations.

Hendon garage (AE)

Coaches operated on routes: 13,113, 183.

Operator	Dates
A & W Omnibus Co. Ltd (A & W Coaches)	October 1947 to by 18th May 1948 and 7th February 1949 to 8th April 1949
Lewis Cronshaw Ltd	23rd October 1947 to 24th June 1949
Curtis and Hearn	21st June 1948 to 27th May 1949
Elms Coaches (H. L. Cheek)	3rd August 1948 to 8th April 1949
Enterprise Coaches (A. W. Latham)	23rd October 1947 to November 1947
Parker's Coaches	21st June 1948 to 8th April 1949
Venture Transport (Hendon) Ltd	18th May 1948 to 27th May 1949

Parker's Coaches of Kingsbury operated only one coach on London Transport services and it was this Tilling Stevens C60A7 with Park Royal body seen here working Route 13 at St Clement Danes Church in the Strand. New to Alexandra Coaches Ltd of Southsea in March 1932 it passed through the hands of G. Ewen (Pioneer) of Petersfield in 1935 and then K. W. Services of Daventry in 1945 before coming to W. R. Parker in April 1948. It looks extremely well turned out for an eighteen year old vehicle with such a history. The route label, partly hidden by the driver's cab, is for the full 13 route from Hendon to London Bridge and, looking at the young gentleman with cutaway collar watching the photographer, one gets the impression that it would have been a very comfortable ride.   J. F. Higham

This 25 seat normal control Commer was Mr H. L. Cheek's sole contribution to the hired coaches scheme and he did not participate until August 1948. Using the fleet name Elms Motors, the coach operated from its base at 384 Kenton Road, Kenton and being petrol engined had to return via Cricklewood garage at the end of the day to refuel since Hendon was an all-diesel garage by the end of 1948. The coach is only recorded as having worked on Route 113 and it is noticeable that the route label only covers the section between Oxford Circus, at which terminus it is seen, and Mill Hill, not serving the northern end of the route to Edgware. The coach appears to have originated in Dorset in 1934. In later years Mr Cheek was to be involved in the operation of Route 98B between Rayners Lane and Ruislip. D. W. K. Jones

Two of Venture Transport's smart Brush bodied AEC Regal coaches stand in The Burroughs outside Hendon garage ready for service on Route 183 between Northwood and Golders Green. At this date Venture, who once ran a London to Luton service, and Lewis Cronshaw's company were rivals for business but in February 1960 Venture was to become a subsidiary of Cronshaw's. D. W. K. Jones

Standing in Babington Road, alongside Hendon garage, Lewis Cronshaw's Leyland Tiger BV4454 is labelled for the 'in-town' section of Route 113 between Oxford Circus and Hendon Central. This solid looking 1935 coach in its cream and maroon livery bears a Blackburn registration which was common on Cronshaw vehicles, the firm originating in that town in 1913 and still having connections there. Being a petrol vehicle this is another coach which would have had to replenish its fuel at a garage other than Hendon at the end of the day. D. W. K. Jones

SME81, the Brush bodied AEC Regal shown in another picture ready for Route 183 has, on this occasion been allocated to the 13 route and although the label on the bulkhead window says 'Hendon and London Bridge' it is obviously working a duty which terminated at Golders Green Station. This is an interesting commentary on Route 13 in 1948 with the hired coach alongside RT 374, one of the new RTs allocated to the route from Cricklewood garage. Hendon however was still soldiering on with its ever reliable STDs on the route and one is lined up behind the coach.   Alan B. Cross

Curtis and Hearn, whose garage was at Milespit Hill, Mill Hill, worked two coaches on London Transport routes. The original one was a pre-war Tilling Stevens but when they received delivery of this Bedford Duple OB in 1948 they put that to work as well. Unusually it is recorded as having a Perkins oil engine. Shy of a fleetname on the side of the body, the Curtis and Hearn name is discreetly shown in gothic lettering in the offside indicator box. It is pulling away while on Route 13 from the St Clement Danes Church stop in Strand with a rather vintage looking taxi behind.   J. F. Higham

Although Lewis Cronshaw's livery is listed as cream and maroon, very little of the darker colour was in evidence on the post-war coaches. These included a pair of Duple bodied Daimler CVD6s, one of which is seen in Babington Road alongside Hendon garage ready for service on Route 13. In similar fashion to the elderly Leyland Tiger shown earlier in this section, a Blackburn registration is carried.   D. W. K. Jones

Holloway garage (J)

Coaches operated on routes: 4A, 14, 19, 27A, 134

Operator	Dates
Camden Coaches	23rd October 1947 to 22nd July 1949
W. J. Carter	21st June 1948 to 8th April 1949
W. Cowell	18th May 1948 to 8th April 1949
Dryer's Coaches Ltd	18th May 1948 to 27th May 1949
Fallowfield & Britten Ltd	November 1947 to 7th February 1949
Frame's Tours Ltd	23rd October 1947 to 5th March 1948
Gatehouse Coaches	3rd August 1948 to 8th April 1949
J. M. Motors	October 1947 to 22nd July 1949
Lawrence Brothers (Transport) Ltd	October 1947 to 24th June 1949
Overland Lismore Coaches Ltd	7th February 1949 to 8th April 1949
Radio Coaches	13th October 1948 to 6th November 1948
Rose Transport Co. Ltd	October 1947 to 22nd July 1949

The once familiar entrance to Holloway garage next to Kingsdown Road in Holloway Road frames this 31 seat Leyland Tiger TS2 belonging to J. M. Motors. Dating from 1932 the bus was delivered new to Hucks Brothers of Burham, Rochester in Kent, which was a piece of local trading since the body is by Short Brothers of the same locality. It passed with Hucks business to Maidstone and District in January 1933 with whom it remained as their fleet number 699 until requisitioned by the Army in July 1940. It came to J. M. Motors in August 1948 but left them for its homeland of Kent by November, going to Marion Coaches of Margate.　D. W. K. Jones

Another of J. M. Motors varied selection of vehicles, which were kept at the Metropolitan Cattle Market situated between York Way and Caledonian Road at Market Road, was this 32 seat Leyland Cheetah dating from 1938. The glasses in the cantrail have been adapted to advertise the possibilities of coach hire from Mr Manuel, who was the 'J. M.' in question and the telephone number 'North 2360' is given, which is so much nicer that the eleven digit number which would be needed today. The coach is standing at the 'Northcote' terminus of the 19 route at Clapham Junction.   D. A. Ruddom collection

It rather looks as though the smiling gentleman (could he be the driver?) has acquired a bottle of the hard stuff nicely packaged in a box. If he is the driver it is to be hoped he will not consume it before taking this venerable Leyland Tiger with Leyland body belonging to J. M. Motors on its journey from Finsbury Park to Clapham Junction on Route 19. New as Ribble No. 625 in 1929 it was withdrawn in 1936, passed to Baker Bros of London, E2 in July 1937 and then to Grey Green in March 1945 before it was acquired by Mr Manuel in January 1947. He passed it on in August 1948. The bus stop in Blackstock Road behind the coach is mounted on one of the old iron posts which looks as if it has seen better days.   Alan B. Cross

While most of Mr Manuel's fleet carried the name 'J. M. Motors' this 1936 Bedford WTB has acquired the rather superior name of 'J. M. Coaches'. The 26 seater was acquired in May 1948 from Birch Brothers for whom it had operated as K56. They in turn had gained it from the 'Perseverence' fleet of F. A. Jenkins of Shillington in 1938. It later went on to be used by Castle Coaches of Lewisham and also Grove Coaches of Harrow. Passengers are alighting from the rear entrance at Hyde Park Corner, while the bowler hatted gentleman scans the horizon for some other bus. Opposite, one of the LTC private hire coaches heads west down Knightsbridge.   J. F. Higham

Elsewhere in this book former C1 can be seen working for Overland Lismore Motors Ltd of Kentish Town on Route 68. They acquired it in May 1948 from J. M. Motors of Holloway who had already operated it out of Holloway garage on Route 19. Here it stands in J. M's livery at the Northcote, Clapham Junction in November 1947 while working the route. It was new in October 1934 with a body built by LPTB at their Chiswick works which was unique to the class. Originally petrol engined it had received a Perkins oil engine in June 1935. It had started its life as a red bus working from Hounslow, then Merton and Barking before transferring to the Country Area at Chelsham, Windsor and St Albans.   V. C. Jones

This photograph illustrates one of the difficulties in establishing firm information about the hired coaches in this period. The photographer recorded the vehicle as being Camden Coaches' Bedford HYF905. The registration is very indistinct but could be taken as that number. However, this number does not appear on any of the London Transport lists of Camden Coaches which have been seen although HYF906 does. It has not been established whether the company had a pair or whether in fact this is HYF906. What is certain is that it is at Victoria working the section of Route 134 between there and Friern Barnet.   J. F. Higham

Not bearing any visible signs of its operator, this Bedford OB with rather unusual bodywork is actually owned by Dryer's Coaches Ltd. Although their registered address was in Wadham Road, Walthamstow, they garaged their vehicles at Flight's Garage in Parkhurst Road, Holloway as did several other operators including Orange Luxury Coaches. This was a hark back to the nineteen-twenties and the days of the independents. Then at least four or five operators housed their buses in the premises. The Bedford shown here is at Twickenham Station on Route 27A and was only offered for use by Dryers on 9th November 1948, which dates the photograph to the latter part of the hired coach period.   J. F. Higham

This imposing Gilford 168SD with Duple bodywork originated in 1930 with Bird Motor Services of Halstead in Essex, so called it is believed because the proprietor, Mr A. Akers was landlord of the 'Bird in Hand' public house. The undertaking passed to Eastern National in December 1934 and this coach was given the fleet number 3502. Now in the ownership of W. Cowell of Islington, another operator who sometimes used Flight's Garage at Holloway, it is at Twickenham Station on the 27A route.   J. F. Higham

The terminus at Oxford Road, Putney was a favourite spot for photographers to record the vehicles on Route 14. Followed by a Holloway STL, this Bedford OB with Duple bus body was new to Lawrence Bros (Transport) Ltd, as clearly shown in the blind box in 1948 although they sold it on in the following year. The firm was more well known for haulage business and operated from Pickard Street, off City Road. Michael Rooum

Hornchurch garage (RD)
Coaches operated on routes: 86A, 123, 175

Operator	Dates
Dagenham Coach Services	12th January 1949 to 19th August 1949
Gidea Park Coaches Ltd	13th October 1948 to 8th April 1949
Harold Wood Coach Services	21st June 1948 to 22nd July 1949
Jays Coaches	3rd August 1948 to 19th August 1949
Leighton Coach Co. Ltd	20th September 1948 to 13th October 1948
R. McCormack	October 1947 to 26th March 1949
Pathfinder Luxury Coaches	21st June 1948 to 24th June 1949

No photographs have been traced showing Hornchurch operations.

Hounslow garage (AV)

Coaches operated on routes: 33, 81, 110, 111, 116, 117, 237

Operator	Dates
Acorn Motors Ltd (Hanworth Coaches)	21st June 1948 to 27th May 1949
Feltham Transport Company	October 1947 to 22nd July 1949
T. E. Garner (Garner's Coaches Ltd)	15th March 1948 to 19th August 1949
Rayner's Coachways Ltd	October 1947 to 19th August 1949
Star Luxury Coaches (Burfoot & Jones)	26th January 1948 to 27th May 1949

Feltham Transport's Gilford Hera stands alongside ST138 at Twickenham Station while both nineteen thirties vehicles are working Route 110 to Hounslow via Powder Mill Lane. The coach, which had a Leyland petrol engine, entered service with W. Alexander & Sons Ltd as their Y50 in May 1934. Three years later it left Scotland and came to Feltham Transport via Rayners Coachways. The body is the typical Wycombe production with the curved window on the nearside of the bulkhead which has proved a useful place to display the route number. J. F. Higham

This 32 seater Albion Valkyrie was new to G. & R. Smollett of Rothienorman in Scotland in May 1934 passing to W. Alexander & Sons Ltd in November 1935. Withdrawn in 1944 it found its way south to join the fleet of Rayner's Coachways of Feltham, Middlesex in July 1945. Rayner's used two addresses to house their coaches during this period. One was at 596 London Road, Ashford while the other was the Baber Bridge Garage in Hounslow Road, Feltham. Since this photograph is dated 1947 it is likely that it is at the former address where the vehicle was found prepared for service between Hounslow and Staines via Feltham on Route 117. The size and rake of the steering wheel is very impressive, although whether the driver thought so after a spell of duty is open to debate. Alan B. Cross

Kingston garage (K)

Coaches operated on routes: 65, 131, 201, 216, 218, 219

Operator	Dates
Acorn Motors Ltd (Hanworth Coaches)	21st June 1948 to 27th May 1949
Blue & White Star Transport Co. Ltd (White Star Coaches)	October 1947 to 19th August 1949
G. J. Futcher (Ace Coaches)	18th May 1948 to 30th October 1948
Hampton Coaches	21st June 1948 to 8th April 1949
Roberts & Dickenson (Ashford Belle and Martindale Coaches)	21st November 1947 to 19th August 1949
Ben Stanley Ltd	24th November 1947 to 24th June 1949

This Leyland TS2 was new to Maidstone & District in 1930 as their fleet number 610 and was one of a number described as 'Pullman saloons'. In February 1937 it was fitted with a new 32 seat Harrington coach body and it was withdrawn in 1941 when it was requisitioned by the Army. Subsequent to the war it was obtained by the Ashford Belle Coaches section of Roberts & Dickenson and continued in service with them until the end of the 1950s. The Leyland radiator has been disguised by the R and D monogram at the top and the coach stands at Kingston Station in September 1948 ready for service to Walton on Route 131.   Alan B. Cross

Four coaches stand ready to assist Kingston garage in the yard adjacent to Kingston Station. KJ1863 in the left foreground is a 1931 Commer 6TK with 20 seat body by the Chatham Motor Company. New in 1931 to Col. J. H. Layton of Gillingham, Kent, who operated under the Medway District Bus Owners' umbrella, it was taken over by Maidstone & District in August 1931. It remained with that company until May 1947 when it passed to its present owner, Roberts and Dickenson. This and the small unidentified coach behind are prepared for the 131, while White Star Coaches JPK871 is destined for the 218 and Ben Stanley's Bedford OWB, JPL163, for the 219 to Weybridge. Two of the operators have taken steps to ensure that the engines are protected from the cold. Alan B. Cross

Blue and White Star Transport, who also operated as 'White Star Coaches', provided three Bedford OWBs for London Transport service. JPK498 waits in the Kingston yard labelled for service on Route 65 from Kingston to Ealing. Kingston garage only had an allocation of four duties on Mondays to Fridays during the period of hired coaches and yet there are several pictures showing Kingston based coaches on the 65. This may have been covering shortages from Turnham Green, who had the major allocation on the route. Alan B. Cross

Numbers 6 and 7 of the Ashford Belle fleet are lined up at Kingston both equipped for duty on Route 65. The 32 seat AEC Regal on the left originated with Huddersfield Corporation in 1934 and first appeared on the London Transport lists during 1948. Its companion, Gilford coach CNO76, was one of the vehicles used by Edward Hillman on his Airways service and had a large luggage compartment, restricting the seating capacity. It passed to British Airways and then BOAC before appearing with Ashford Belle in 1948. The Ashford Belle coaches were kept in Bentall's Garage in Wood Street, Kingston.   Alan B. Cross

Ben Stanley's Coaches was one operator who had a fairly lengthy approved run from its base in Burwood Road, Hersham to the London Transport garage at Kingston. Three Bedford OWBs were used and this one, parked at Kingston alongside Ashford Belle's Leyland Lion, is ready for service on Route 219 to Weybridge via Hersham, very much its home territory.   D. A. Ruddom collection

Blue and White Star Coaches operated three Bedford OWBs on
London Transport services from
Kingston and they carried the 'White
Star Coaches' fleet name. This view
in the Kingston Station yard shows
that varying liveries were also used.
The somewhat exotic streamlining
of the livery on the nearest vehicle
seems out of keeping with the
functional lines of the bodywork and
is a little reminiscent of Kingston
upon Hull practice rather than
Kingston upon Thames. It is labelled
for the 218 from Kingston to
Staines via Laleham and
presumably the Bedford OWB is
compatible with the weight restric-
tion on Walton Bridge, which the
route used. Alan B. Cross

Acorn Motors Ltd, who also operated as Hanworth Coaches, supplied AKL472, a Dennis Lancet with a Duple
deck and a half body, during 1948. New to Auto Pilots of Folkestone in 1933, it passed to East Kent in December
1935. It must have been a different experience for the conductor allocated to work the vehicle. It stands in
Cromwell Road at Kingston outside the site of the shops which nowadays include the 'Smokebox' familiar to
transport enthusiasts. The number displayed in the bulkhead window indicates its use on Route 216, the more
direct road to Staines via Ashford. Alan B. Cross

This Dennis Lancet, belonging to Acorn Motors, carries a Middlesex registration – LMY645 – which was issued no earlier than 1946. The coach however, with a radiator design dating between 1931 and 1936, appears to be much older and has doubtless been re-registered. As can be seen from the list at the start of this section, Kingston garage utilised the coaches on most of their routes. This one is set for Route 201 which in 1948 was running from Feltham Station to Kingston via Hanworth, Teddington, Hampton Court, Thames Ditton, Long Ditton and Surbiton.   Alan B. Cross

Wycombe bodies are usually associated with Gilford chassis but when the origins of this Dennis Lancet are realised it is perhaps easier to understand how this 1932 combination came about. The bus was new to the Penn Bus Company, who operated in the High Wycombe area, so it was a case of local industry being patronised. When the company was wound up in 1935 this Dennis passed to Thames Valley. By 1948 it had found its way to Acorn Motors as seen here and it appeared on Route 65.   Alan B. Cross

Leyton garage (T)

Coaches operated on routes: 35, 38, 38A. 236

Operator	Dates
Advance Motor Services (A. Clark & Sons)	18th May 1948 to 8th April 1949
Classique Coaches Ltd	October 1947 to 19th August 1949
Essex County Coaches	23rd October 1947 to by 18th May 1948 and
	13th October 1948 to 27th May 1949
Majestic Luxury Coaches Ltd	October 1947 to February 1948 and by
	21st June 1948 to 8th April 1949
Sunbeam (C. J. Worsley)	October 1947 to 27th May 1949
Thorpe Coaches Ltd	23rd October 1947 to 18th May 1948
Winwood Coaches Ltd	October 1947 to 22nd July 1949

This London registered 1931 AEC Regal, although never being a part of the London Transport fleet, conveniently carries a destination blind box which fits a contemporary LT blind and so a proper destination can be displayed. Owned by Sunbeam, the Walthamstow firm of C. J. Worsley, it served throughout the hired coach period. The hired coaches on the 38A route were all based at Leyton garage and none operated out of Loughton.
Alan B. Cross

This elegant Maudslay coach of 1931 belongs to Classique Coaches Ltd of Lea Bridge Road, Leyton and is working on Route 35 between Camberwell Green and Chingford Hatch. Four such coaches were owned by Classique, certainly meriting their name, and they all carried Essex registrations. This one is EV943 and the others were EV942 and EV423 and 424. The glass weathershields above the windows are all intact, something that could rarely be said for the contemporary single deck LTs of London Transport.   J. F. Higham

Aldershot & District D 437 (BOT288) was new in December 1936 and was requisitioned by the War Department from 1940 onwards. Subseqently re-registered, this Dennis Lancet now belongs to Thorpe Coaches of Ilford. Thorpe garaged their vehicles in Leyton High Road adjoining the Ritz Cinema but despite their proximity to Leyton garage they worked from there only in the earlier half of the hired coach period. This solid looking Strachan bodied coach is followed by a gleaming new RT, while the rest of Victoria Station forecourt is inhabited by STLs.   J. F. Higham

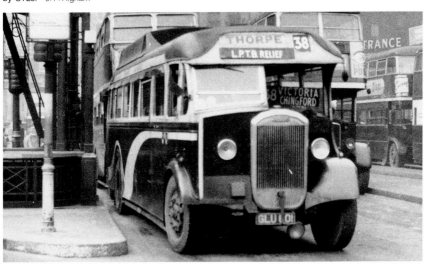

Another of Thorpe Coaches' Dennis Lancets, EXO797 dating from 1938, carried this full fronted Duple body with streamlining typical of the age in which it was built. One always felt that the driver's vision was somewhat restricted with this style, particularly when doing this type of work involving accurately drawing in to bus stops. This is another instance where the cramped entrance and exit availability is clearly seen, which must have increased 'dwell time' at stops considerably. Working from Leyton on Route 38 at Victoria, it is flanked by the new and old order – an RT to the front and an LT to the rear.   Alan B. Cross

GH3817 was formerly T 194, a Green Line coach delivered in September 1930 with a body by Short Brothers of Rochester and allocated to Bishops Stortford garage. It was one of the first to be disposed of by the Board in May 1938 and was initially sold to Lancashire Motor Traders of Knott Mill. Eventually it found its way to Sunbeam of Walthamstow for whom it is working here at Victoria on Route 38A. J. F. Higham

Loughton garage (L)
No hired coaches operated from this garage.

Merton garage (AL)

Coaches operated on routes: 88, 118, 156

Operator	Dates
L. C. Davis & Sons Ltd	23rd October 1947 to 27th May 1949
United Service Transport Co. Ltd (including Blue Belle Motors Ltd and L. Adnams)	October 1947 to 27th May 1949

On 7th February 1949 two of United Service's own fleet of Leyland Tiger PS1s, with United's curious AEC style triangle to denote ownership on the radiator, stand outside Morden Station on hired coach duties from Merton garage. That on the left is working the 118, which at the time ran from Raynes Park to Clapham Common, while the one on the right is working on the additional shuttle service which ran across the ostensible 'terminus' of the circular 156 route from North Cheam (Queen Victoria) to St Helier Avenue. The main allocation on the 156 route was from Sutton garage, as exemplified by the Daimler in the background, but at this date Merton had a small weekday commitment.   Alan B. Cross

DPU90 was new to Essex County Coaches of London, E15 in 1936. The AEC Regal now belongs to L. C. Davis and Sons of Streatham and is working on the 88 route from Merton garage. In 1936 Duple began to offer a style of coach body with curved driver's windscreen but this example represents the rather more traditional straight cab which was still available and nonetheless attractive. The London Transport lists seemed uncertain over the period as to whether this coach seated 32 or 35 passengers but it is thought the former is correct. J. F. Higham

Middle Row garage (X)

Coaches operated on routes: 7A, 15, 28

Operator	Dates
Fred Davis & Sons (Roseland)	October 1947 to 27th May 1949
Orange Coaches (Keith & Boyle) Ltd	23rd October 1947 to 13th October 1948
Paddington Transport Services Ltd	October 1947 to 24th June 1949
Red Line Continental Motorways Ltd	October 1947 to 8th April 1949

Fred Davis and Sons had their garage at 9 Roseland Place, off the Portobello Road, hence the use of the fleet name 'Roseland'. Their London Transport work was confined to operation from the nearby Middle Row garage and Fred Davis operated three coaches in the scheme. One was a Commer, one a Dennis and the third was this Wycombe bodied Gilford dating from 1934/35. It stands at the top of London Bridge Street while working the 7A to East Acton on a rather murky 11th February 1948. Alan B. Cross

Paddington Transport Services Ltd was another company who used an odd assortment of rather aged coaches, in their case an ex-London Transport T (T 363), a Gilford Hera and this Leyland LZ2 32-seat full fronted coach which originated with Scottish Motor Traction. Close examination shows that the seats were fairly closely spaced and the City commuters have begun to take their places for the ride across the bridge into work from London Bridge Station. Although not dated, this must be a 1949 scene as one of Hammersmith garage's new RTLs is parked behind on the 17 route and will follow the coach all the way to Marble Arch. J. F. Higham

This Orange Luxury Coaches Bedford Duple coach has been included under Middle Row garage since it is clearly dressed for work on the 15 between Ladbroke Grove and East Ham. Why it is parked alongside Victoria garage in Guildhouse Street is not certain. Orange did work on four routes out of Victoria garage so maybe it is about to have its label changed. Nevertheless Orange was the only one of the four companies working from Middle Row that did not have any pre-war vehicles and these coaches always did give a very pleasant ride. It appears that some of their vehicles were given names and this one's offside wing tells us that it (or she) is Ella. D. W. K. Jones

Mortlake garage (M)

Coaches operated on routes: 9, 73

Operator	Dates
L. C. Davis & Sons	October 1947 to by June 1948
Empress Coaches (J. G. Green)	18th May 1948 to 22nd July 1949
Golden Miller Coaches	October 1947 to 22nd July 1949
Mountain Transport Services Ltd	18th May 1948 to 24th June 1949
United Service Transport Co. Ltd (including Blue Belle Motors Ltd and L. Adnams)	23rd October 1947 to 18th May 1948

Fifty odd years on and Golden Miller, under the guise of Telling's Golden Miller, is once again operating London Transport bus services. In 1948 their immaculate new Bedford Duple, SMY152 heads inwards from Mortlake with a very respectable load. Once again this is one of those pictures which exudes the atmosphere of 1948, with the style of dress, the design of the pram and the lack of traffic or road markings.
Michael Rooum

Mountain Transport Services of Maresa Road, Chelsea were notable (notorious might be a better word!) for running ex-Trent SOS single deckers in the scheme and these are illustrated elsewhere in this book. In spring 1949 however they obtained and put into service on Route 9 a new Austin CXB coach which really did uplift their image. Here it is caught at St Clement Danes Church in the Strand gleaming its way along, complete with the London Transport bullseye fixed to the radiator. These were issued in the latter part of the period and replaced the various London Transport labels previously used.   J. F. Higham

Muswell Hill garage (MH)

Coaches operated on routes: 43, 212, 244

Operator	Dates
Crouch End Luxury (J. Hanslip Broadway Coaches)	October 1947 to 22nd July 1949
Grey Green Coaches	14th February 1949 to 27th May 1949
Horseshoe Coaches	October 1947 to 24th June 1949
Viney's Luxury Coaches	13th October 1948 to 22nd July 1949
White Line Coaches	24th November 1947 to 24th June 1949

This 32-seat Leyland Tiger, with central entrance bodywork by Petty, dates from 1932 and has arrived at Finsbury Park in Stroud Green Road before turning into Wells Terrace. It is in the blue and black livery of Horseshoe Coaches whose garage was at Culross Road, West Green. For a vehicle in its sixteenth year it seems to be very well maintained and preserved.   D. W. K. Jones

Crouch End Luxury in grey and maroon livery were always a very smart outfit in the early post-war years and one of their Duple bodied AEC Regals is on the stand at the 'Orange Tree', Friern Barnet with the Town Hall in the background. The Town Hall was still relatively new, only being completed at the start of World War II. The picture will have been taken in 1949 since behind the coach is RT 1152, the first of the Saunders RTs delivered to Muswell Hill in January. The pole on the island, still wearing its wartime black and white stripes, held a plunger which conductors of buses leaving the stand could strike to activate the traffic lights at the immediate junction. In its way this was an early form of traffic priority for buses.   D. W. K. Jones

This smart blue and black liveried Bedford OB/Duple coach of Horseshoe Coaches was more regularly employed on the 212 route but here it is at London Bridge on the 43 to Friern Barnet. It always seemed to be in the hands of one particular driver, as recalled in the book *Routes to Recovery.*   J. F. Higham

Norwood garage (N)

Coaches operated on routes: 2, 3, 68

Operator	Dates
Castle Coaches (C. C. Grundon)	October 1947 to by 18th May 1948
Grove Coaches (H. R. B. Shugg)	23rd October 1947 to 19th August 1949
Thorne Brothers	October 1947 to 22nd July 1949
United Service Transport Co. Ltd (including Blue Belle Motors Ltd and L. Adnams)	October 1947 (?) and 13th October 1948 to 27th May 1949
Woodside Coaches	3rd August 1948 to 27th May 1949

This 1932 Daimler belonging to Mr Shugg's Grove Coaches stands outside the National Gallery waiting to begin its journey from this point to Crystal Palace on Route 3. Thirty-two seats were provided in this vehicle which appears to be extremely well kept. The radiator surround and headlamps would do the firm credit in any rally of preserved vehicles today.   J. F. Higham

This rather ponderous looking Dennis Lancet dates from 1938 and is being used by Thorne Brothers of Brixton Hill on the 68 route out of Norwood garage. In the murky darkness under the canopy it can be discerned that it is fitted for working the Upper Norwood (Beulah Spa) to Kings Cross shorts, which were a regular feature of the 68 at this time.   Alan B. Cross

Nunhead garage (AH)

Coaches operated on routes: 12, 63, 78

Operator	Dates
Ansell's Coaches (S. Ansell & Co.; New Karrymore Coaches Ltd)	October 1947 to 19th August 1949
Argosy Super Coaches (F. W. B. Smith)	October 1947 to 22nd July 1949
Charles W. Banfield	April 1948 to 22nd July 1949
Harrison and Hole (H. G. Harrison)	21st June 1948 to 8th April 1949

There are several views in this book of these Leyland LZ2 Cheetahs with full fronted bodies that emanated from Scottish Motor Traction and were used by quite a few of the London area coach operators. It is therefore interesting to see what the rear end looked like. New Karrymore Coaches Ltd was part of Ansell's Coaches with premises in Peckham and Camberwell.   J. F. Higham

This Duple OB is listed as being only a 26-seat version and it looks a little different by virtue of the visor that has been added above the windscreen. 'A. C. Ltd' is in fact Ansell's Coaches Ltd and it is running under the parent company name rather than 'New Karrymore Coaches Ltd'. It is working Route 12 and has arrived at Oxford Circus, the terminus indicated. J. F. Higham

The Stockport registration, JA8865, of Argosy Super Coaches' Bedford WTB dates from 1937. Although the label on the side is for the full extent of Route 63 from Kings Cross to Honor Oak it is obviously coming off service and turning left at Peckham Rye to run into Nunhead garage. The conductor has his ticket box firmly tucked under his arm and is ready to leap off at the earliest opportunity. The King's Arms public house behind suffered war damage and in 1948 had not yet been rebuilt.   W. J. Haynes

This petrol engined Leyland Tiger TS3 of Charles W. Banfield was first registered in 1931 in Essex and appears to still retain its original Leyland built body. It is standing at the Shoreditch Church terminus of Route 78 and behind is an STL from Dalston also working the route. Gas street lights such as that protruding above the roof were still commonplace at this time.   J. F. Higham

Old Kent Road garage (P)

Coaches operated on routes: 21, 53A

Operator	Dates
Ansell's Coaches	18th May 1948 to 21st June 1948
Charles W. Banfield	23rd October 1947 to 22nd July 1949
Elms Longman Motor Services Ltd	18th May 1948 to 22nd July 1949
Harrison & Hole (H. G. Harrison)	18th May 1948 to 21st June 1948
A. R. Holder & Sons Ltd	21st June 1948 to 8th April 1949
C. G. Lewis (Lewis's Safety Coaches)	23rd October 1947 to 22nd July 1949

One of C. G. Lewis's new Duple bodied Maudslay Marathon II coaches is held up by the policeman on point duty, presumably in the vicinity of London Bridge although it does not appear to be on the usual route as it works the 21 between London Bridge and Lewisham. Behind the conductor of the ST on Route 8A takes the opportunity of the hold up to do the usual waving exercise to assist his driver re-set the destination blind, necessary since periscopes were not provided on these vehicles.   J. F. Higham

Elms Longman Motor Services operated this former London Transport vehicle on Route 53A, although there is little or no visible indication of just how much of the route it is working in this view taken in the northern end of Regent Street on 20th July 1948. T127 was first delivered with a Short Brothers body and entered service in July 1930 at Romford on Green Line work. It was one of the first to be disposed of by the Board and passed to Lancashire Motor Traders in May 1938. It has not been ascertained when it received this body, which looks to be older than 1938.   Alan B. Cross

Two coaches stand alongside the bombsites which surrounded Old Kent Road garage, both ready for service on Route 53A. HV484 belonging to Elms Longman Transport Services is labelled for the complete route from Plumstead Common to Camden Town while the unidentified coach behind is ready for short working between Blackheath (Westcombe Hill) and Oxford Circus. Close examination of the cab of this Tilling Stevens shows no sign of the back of the driver's seat but an extremely high and large steering wheel, proving how physically demanding some of these vehicles were to drive.   D. W. K. Jones

Harrison and Hole, who kept their vehicles at the S and S Motor Garage in Harders Road, Peckham, had a very short-lived association with Old Kent Road garage. This 1935 centre entrance Dennis Lancet became available for London Transport service during 1948 and stands in Bowles Road outside Old Kent Road garage billed for Route 53A but with no terminal details.   D. W. K. Jones

Another of the wartime fleet replacements obtained by Mr Lewis of Lewis's Safety Coaches of Greenwich was this Leyland Tiger which originated with Bailey of Dalston in 1932. A very enterprising use has been made of the destination boxes to enable a proper display.   J. F. Higham

Palmers Green garage (AD)

Coaches operated on routes: 34, 102, 112

Operator	Dates
Elms, Phillips and Brown	October 1947 to 8th April 1949
Henry Saloon Coaches Ltd	October 1947 to 22nd July 1949
Lily Coaches	23rd October 1947 to 22nd July 1949
Modern Super Coaches	24th November 1947 to 18th May 1948
Universal Coaches Ltd	October 1947 and February 1948 to 24th June 1949

Universal Coaches of Edmonton eventually became part of the Grey Green empire. However in 1948 they were still independent and supplied this Bedford OWB for operation from Palmers Green garage. Standing outside that garage it displays a rather crumpled bill in its destination box together with what look like 'home made' destination boards, nonetheless effective for that. The metal London Transport bullseye is fixed to the radiator grille. Under the Dalston section of this book the point was made that the Bedford OWB operated by Boughton's appeared to have come from this company and a comparison of the fleet names supports this.   D. W. K. Jones

Henry Saloon Coaches of Tottenham provided a mixed fleet of ancient and modern 'Super Saloons', as the cantrail would have it, for the London Transport services. Although in sparkling condition, this Daimler is one of the more venerable of the fleet carrying a Chester registration from around 1930. It is standing in Regents Avenue outside Palmers Green garage labelled for the 34 route. The coaches did not carry any London Transport running or duty numbers and so it is not certain what the significance is of the '25' displayed in the cab window.   D. W. K. Jones

Plumstead garage (AM)

Coaches operated on routes: 53, 53A

Operator	Dates
Bradshaw's Super Coaches Ltd	27th October 1947 to 27th May 1949
RACS (Royal Arsenal Co-operative Society)	October 1947 and 13th October 1948 to 8th April 1949
Wayfarer Coaches	21st June 1948 to 23rd January 1949

Plumstead garage was one of the lesser users of hired coaches and restricted their use to the 53 and 53A routes, no record being found of them operating on the more localised routes such as 99 or 122. Bradshaw's Bedford Duple OB lays over on the north side of Trafalgar Square along with several other hired vehicles on this quiet and rather misty day. This particular coach left Bradshaw's in November 1948 and then carved out a career for itself in Wales until 1960. J. F. Higham

Potters Bar garage (PB)

Coaches operated on routes: 134

Operator	Dates
Lee's Luxury Coaches Ltd	October 1947 to 27th May 1949

From a selection of three coaches, two AEC and one Dennis, Lee's Luxury Coaches of Barnet supplied one coach on most days during the period for use on the 134 route which at the time ran at its fullest extent from Potters Bar to Pimlico. This coach was bought new by Lee's in 1936 and Alan Townsin in his book on AEC Regals makes the comment that this style of body was the more conservative available from Duple at that date. Nevertheless it gave very good service and this author can vouch for its comfortable ride. One oddity of Lee's operation was that their coaches displayed bills for Potters Bar L.T. Garage and Highgate but the coach regularly worked through to Victoria where it is seen here.
Alan B. Cross

The post-war coach from Lee's trio of vehicles was this Dennis Lancet III with Duple body. It has arrived at the bus stop opposite the 'Orange Tree' at Friern Barnet with a good load of passengers. Waiting for a southbound bus at this point was always a lottery since you could never be quite sure whether one would appear from this direction before the one waiting on the stand, situated just beyond this stop, would leave. D. W. K. Jones

Putney Bridge garage (F)

Coaches operated on routes: 14, 74, 93, 96

Operator	Dates
L. C. Davis & Sons Ltd	23rd October 1947 to 27th May 1949
Empress Coaches (J. G. Green)	21st June 1948 to 27th May 1949
Garner's Coaches Ltd	Not on any lists but photographic evidence exists
Ivanhoe Coaches	7th February 1949 to 8th April 1949
Mountain Transport Services Ltd	12th April 1948 to 8th April 1949
Sceptre Coaches (Bingley Brothers Ltd)	7th February 1949 to 8th April 1949
United Service Transport Co. Ltd (including Blue Belle Motors Ltd and L. Adnams)	October 1947 to 27th May 1949

This 1929 Leyland TS1 with Wadham body was new to Western SMT as their 152 and was the only coach operated on London Transport services by Ivanhoe Coaches, having been procured by them in June 1948. The somewhat fanciful name derives from the fact that the registered address of the company was the Ivanhoe Hotel, Camberwell although the coach was garaged at Hammersmith. Mr J. M. Reeves, displayed above the destination, was listed as purchasing the coach and possibly was the landlord of this hostelry. Most of the time it worked from Hammersmith garage but in the first few months of 1949 it transferred to Putney Bridge in whose yard it is seen. Although labelled for Route 74, the destination blind that has been inserted reads 'LONDON BDG' which is probably a hangover from its days on Route 17. In May 1949 Mr Reeves disposed of the coach to R. Britton Luxury (!) Coaches, presumably having no further use for it when the LT contract ceased. Michael Rooum

A new Commer Q4 chassis fitted with a secondhand body from a Bedford OWB was presented by Mountain Transport Services Ltd of Chiswick Works for inspection as to its suitability in October 1948. Duly accepted, it is seen ready from service for Putney Bridge garage on route 74. Michael Rooum

WH8650 was a 1937 AEC coach with Watson body and was new to Snaylam of Bolton. It arrived with L. C. Davis & Sons Ltd of Streatham after service with Ribble, the Ministry of Transport and the U.S. Army. It is seen parked in the yard at the back of Putney Bridge garage between duties on Route 14. Notable are the rather unusual glass rainshields, which must have been an expensive item to replace in the event of a mishap and are a remarkable survival after such a chequered career, assuming that they are original.   Michael Rooum

L.C. Davis had a small fleet of post-war Bedford Duple OBs, as did most coach operators at the time, and this one – MME 744 – is in the Putney Bridge yard allocated to the 74 route from Putney Heath to Camden Town (the 'Zoo bus'). As will be seen from this selection of photographs, Davis operated on a wide selection of routes covering many areas of London and his drivers needed to be pretty familiar with the geography of the capital.   Michael Rooum

Mountain Transport are best remembered for the four ex-Trent Motor Traction Co Ltd SOS single deckers with Brush bodies which they ran on London Transport routes. Dating from 1932 these vehicles always gave the impression to London tuned eyes of being much older, especially if you consider that they were actually younger than the single deck LTs or the 7T7 Green Line coaches. From a ride on one, it is remembered that the one modernity appeared to be a bell rope running the length of the saloon. This fine view shows RC410 prepared for service on Route 74 but they also ventured on to the 96 and, while at Mortlake garage, the 9.   K. W. Glazier collection

Another of L.C. Davis's collection of AECs was this Regent which dates from 1932 according to its Swansea registration. The Harrington coach body is obviously a later addition to the double deck marque of chassis. Also photographed in the Putney Bridge yard, this one is earmarked for use on the 96 route, which in 1948 ran from Putney Common to Redbridge Station, a route which disappeared in the 1958 cuts. Michael Rooum

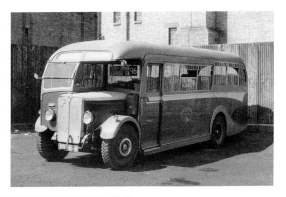

Empress Coaches of Fulham initially worked from Hammersmith and Mortlake garages but in June 1948 added some Putney Bridge duties to their portfolio. DF8186, a 1931 petrol engined Leyland Tiger TS2 with London Lorries body had been owned by Empress since May 1939. It is parked at the Putney Bridge yard and the route description appears to have been doctored to omit the Heath from the Putney Heath destination. Michael Rooum

Another Bedford Duple OB was supplied to Route 14 by L. Adnams, part of the United Service Transport combine, and this nearside view complements that of the Sceptre Coaches example shown working the same route on the cover. The normal control layout may seem profligate in this age of underfloor engines but there is no doubt that aesthetically these were lovely coaches that gave a quiet comfortable ride. Michael Rooum

Seven Kings garage (AP)

Coaches operated on routes: 25A, 139, 148

Operator	Dates
Avondale Safety Coaches (Tatnall Bros Ltd)	October 1947 to 22nd July 1949
Bontonian Coaches	21st June 1948 to 8th April 1949
Dagenham Coach Services	24th November 1947 to 11th January 1949
Dix Luxury Coaches	October 1947 to 23rd January 1949
Leighton Coach Company Ltd	October 1947 and 18th May 1948 to 19th August 1949
Pathfinder Luxury Coaches	23rd October 1947 to 23rd January 1949

There are plenty of passengers waiting to cram into this Bedford OWB of the Leighton Coach Company for the ride down to Ilford and beyond as it helps out on Route 148. In the background an open staircase LT can be seen negotiating the Gants Hill roundabout. Note the bells of the inspectors' telephone mounted below the bus stop flag and the British Railways lorry parked over on the wrong side of Cranbrook Road. Alan B. Cross

Despite its seeming bulk, this 1932 Hertfordshire registered AEC Regal, previously with Hull Brothers, only seats 32 passengers in its Petty built body. Avondale Safety Coaches operated from Becontree Avenue, Dagenham and so the environment of the Becontree Estate, through which the 148 ran, was quite familiar territory. The photo is dated 23rd June 1949. Alan B. Cross

Shepherds Bush garage (S)

Coaches operated on routes: 12, 105

Operator	Dates
Clifton and Kalber	June 1948 to 13th October 1948
Progress Coaches (A. E. Fox)	21st June 1948 to 22nd July 1949
Smith's Luxury Coaches	9th August 1948 to 24th June 1949
Ubique Coaches	18th May 1948 to 24th June 1949
Venture Transport (Hendon) Ltd	23rd October 1947 to 21st June 1948

Upper right This former Scottish Motor Traction Leyland Cheetah, one of a small fleet owned by Smith's, was presented for inspection by London Transport only on 2nd November 1948 so its LT service was relatively limited. Above the windows it proudly announces 'Daily Services to Southsea, Bognor and Littlehampton, Southampton and Portsmouth, Brighton and Worthing'. More prosaically the front blind reads 'Shepherds Bush 12'. The rear entrance with door and railed luggage rack on the roof above have almost an African air about them.   D. W. K. Jones

Sidcup garage (SP)

Coaches operated on routes: 21, 21A, 132, 161, 241

Operator	Dates
Fred G. Atkins	21st June 1948 to 8th April 1949
Bexleyheath Transport Co. Ltd	October 1947 to 22nd July 1949
P. Currie Ltd	21st June 1948 to 24th June 1949
W. E. Grundon	23rd October 1947 to 19th August 1949

Lower right GF1737 was one of a trio of AEC Regals with Harrington bodies purchased in March 1930 by Edward Paul Ltd of Forest Hill who up until January 1928 had operated bus services as a London independent. At the beginning of the war the three AECs passed to Valliant Direct Coaches Ltd of Ealing and this one passed on to W. E. Grundon of Eltham in July 1946. Eventually it was withdrawn in April 1951 but not before it had worked for London Transport from Sidcup garage. It stands at Eltham with a neatly inserted London Transport blind showing the Sidcup destination.   D. W. K. Jones

Streatham garage (AK)

Coaches operated on routes: 133

Operator	Dates
Argosy Super Coaches	October 1947 to by 18th May 1948
John Bennett (Croydon) Ltd	13th October 1948 to 27th May 1949
L. C. Davis & Sons Ltd	18th May 1948 to 22nd July 1949
L. Manny Ltd	21st June 1948 to 8th April 1949
R.A.C.S. (Royal Arsenal Co-operative Society)	13th October 1948 to 27th May 1949
Streatham Vale Luxury Coaches	23rd October 1947 to 24th June 1949
W. Watkins	19th May 1948 to June 1948

No photographs have been traced showing Streatham operations.

Sutton garage (A)

Coaches operated on routes: 93, 151, 156, 213

Operator	Dates
John Bennett (Croydon) Ltd	October 1947 to 18th May 1948
Carshalton & Wallington Coaches Ltd	23rd October 1947 to 19th August 1949
A. P. Down	24th November 1947 to 24th June 1949
H. J. Sargent	18th May 1948 to 22nd July 1949

G. Lambird's Carshalton and Wallington Coaches possessed this 1933 Duple bodied AEC Regal, which is seen working a short section of the 93 route between North Cheam and Wimbledon only. It was originally bought by Bingley Brothers of Hammersmith for their Sceptre Coaches operation. Although fifteen years old and come through the war years, the coach looks in remarkably good condition. It is indicative of the care that smaller operators took of their vehicles, knowing that they had to last if the company was to survive. Alan B. Cross

Two of Carshalton and Wallington Coaches' vehicles stand side by side at Morden Station while working Route 93 in contrasting liveries. Nearest the camera in the light version is Bedford OWB LMG 484. It would appear to have gained upholstered seating, although this type of vehicle was delivered in the war years with wooden slatted seats. Alan B. Cross

This 29-seat Bedford OB was the solitary coach provided by A. P. Down whose registered address was Langley Avenue, Worcester Park but who used the aptly named Langley Garage at 118 London Road, North Cheam to house the vehicle. Standing outside Morden Station on 20th May 1948 there is no route number in evidence but the nearside blind reads 'NORTH CHEAM QUEEN VIC' and underneath 'THE WOODSTOCK'. This does not appear to be a London Transport blind and just why Mr Down should have such a display is a little unclear. However, it was reasonably useful for either Route 93 or 156 if a little ambiguous.   Alan B. Cross

Of the three Bedford OWBs supplied by Sargent's of East Grinstead and garaged at Croydon during the latter half of the hired coach period, one worked from Sutton. On 25th May 1948, just a week after they commenced, fleet number 01 is carrying out that duty on the 156 'swingers' from North Cheam to St Helier Avenue which worked across the nominal terminal point of this circular route at Morden Station. It appears to be a 'flag day' but the lady on the pavement is not attracting any donors, least of all the lady on the right who may have used the coach as a shield from the rattling tin.   Alan B. Cross

Tottenham garage (AR)

Coaches operated on routes: 41, 73, 76

Operator	Dates
Ardley Brothers Ltd	October 1947 and 26th January 1948 to 24th June 1949
Black & White Coaches Ltd (Davis Luxury Coach)	October 1947 to 19th August 1949
Champion Coaches	October 1947 to 22nd July 1949
Dawson (of Walthamstow)	Listed October 1947 but doubtful if ever operated
Elms, Phillips and Brown	By November 1947 to 27th May 1949
Essex County Coaches	February 1948 to by 18th May 1948 and 13th October 1948 to 7th February 1949
Fallowfield & Britten Ltd	February 1948 to 27th May 1949
Golden Star Coaches Ltd	18th May 1948 to 8th April 1949
Grey Green Coaches	23rd October 1947 to 27th May 1949
P. Hearn	7th February 1949 to 24th June 1949
Henry Saloon Coaches Ltd	26th January 1948 to by 18th May 1948
Lily Coaches	23rd October 1947 to February 1948
Majestic Luxury Coaches Ltd	4th February 1948 to by 18th May 1948
Radio Coaches	18th May 1948 to 24th June 1949
Safeway Coaches	October 1947 to November 1947
S. V. Twigg (County Coaches)	21st June 1948 to 8th April 1949
Universal Coaches Ltd	23rd October 1947 to 4th February 1948

While the many coach operators working from Tottenham garage proliferated on Routes 73 and 76, Radio Coaches were the only company for which there is a record of operation on the suburban Route 41 between Archway and Tottenham Hale. There was a peak hour extension at this time to Ilford but it is unclear whether the coach ever worked beyond Tottenham Hale. In the drab surroundings of the Brookside Road stand at the Archway, this 1947 Maudslay Marathon coach is followed by two of London Transport's rather more elderly allocation to this route. Further down a new RT stands which at this date is probably turning short on Route 134. *Alan B. Cross*

The solid, yet elegant lines of this Duple bodied 1938 Leyland Tiger in the blue livery of Henry's Saloon Coaches are excellently portrayed in this picture. Most of the work that this Tottenham company did for London Transport was from Palmers Green garage but for a few months at the start of 1948 they provided two coaches to assist at Tottenham. Working the East Sheen to Stoke Newington section of Route 73 the coach is followed by a 'Bluebird' LT, a familiar sight on this route at the time.   D. W. K. Jones

While the glass rainshields along the side of this Black & White coach, with the Davis name above the cab, advertise 'Daily Services to the South Coast', the nearest it will get on this day will be East Sheen on London Transport Route 73. Numbered 31 in the Black & White fleet, this Leyland Tiger 32-seater was first registered in London in March 1933 and was a part of the Grey Green Coaches fleet. The fleet name seems to owe something to the roundel logo and the circle gives the telephone number of the company, Larkswood 3331/2/3. Michael Rooum

This elderly Gilford of Champion Coaches also appears in the section under Enfield garage where it is working Route 135. It appears to have received a different livery at some time between the two photographs. Here it has arrived at Tottenham garage, presumably at the end of its duty, and stands in Philip Lane opposite the garage. The conductor waits to have his picture taken, ticket box under arm ready to cross the road and pay in his takings, while another conductor complete with Bell Punch appears to view the coach with some incredulity. A rather 'home made' route number and destination has been provided in the bulkhead window.   D. W. K. Jones

Elms, Phillips and Brown were another Tottenham coach company and appropriately enough they provided one coach to the local London Transport garage. Their Gilford 168 OT with Wycombe body was new to W. Alexander & Sons Ltd as their Y35 in April 1933. Elms obtained it when withdrawn in 1937 but during the war it worked for a Staffordshire operator, returning to Elms in May 1945. It works Route 76 at Victoria alongside LT 1400 working Route 29 from West Green garage. It was very unusual to find a 'Bluebird' LT working from that garage but this one was allocated there on 5th March 1948 to work out its last three months.   Alan B. Cross

This AEC Regal, GF5249, also at Victoria on Route 76, begs a question. Its London registration was never a London Transport one, but the coach does bear some resemblance to a 7T7, although the front nearside bulkhead does not seem to conform. This is Davis (Black & White) number 21 and elsewhere in this book we see their number 22, ex-T 222, with a body which does not resemble a 7T7. Ron Lunn recorded this body as built by Beadle but at the time of writing this caption we had not yet found the answer to exactly what transpired to produce the vehicles illustrated. A body swop appears to have occurred at some stage.
Alan B. Cross

Turnham Green garage (V)

Coaches operated on routes: 65, 91

Operator	Dates
Cosy Coaches	3rd August 1948 to 22nd July 1949
Garner's Coaches Ltd (also t/a Hounslow Star)	23rd October 1947 to 19th August 1949

This petrol engined Dennis Lancet, with a Leicester registration dating from 1932, belongs to R. E. Nealon's 'Cosy Coaches' fleet and no doubt as it trundled along the interior could be quite cosy. Strangely that is not an image that any coach operator today would particularly espouse. It is standing outside Turnham Green garage in Belmont Road, while in the background a new RT off the 91 turns into the shed, and across the road a fleet of Garner's Bedford OBs are lined up ready for work.   D. W. K. Jones

Garner's Coaches Ltd, whose garage was at 174 High Street, Hounslow, also used the fleet name 'Hounslow Star' as seen on this Bedford OB. It was one of a number owned by Garner, who in the winter of 1947/8 were operating no fewer than eleven coaches from Turnham Green garage. The six Bedford OBs registered MMT861-866 are recorded as being 27-seat vehicles, presumably having a little more leg room. This one is ready for service on the 65 between Ealing and Hook. D. W. K. Jones

Twickenham garage (AB)

Coaches operated on route: 27A

Operator	Dates
Feltham Transport Company	Photographic evidence but not on any lists seen
Garner's Coaches Ltd (also t/a Hounslow Star)	23rd October 1947 to 18th May 1948 and
	13th October 1948 to 27th May 1949
Red Line Continental Motorways Ltd	23rd October 1947 to 18th May 1948
Roberts & Dickenson (Ashford Belle and Martindale Coaches)	18th May 1948 to 19th August 1949

Roberts & Dickenson of Kingston traded as both Ashford Belle and Martindale Coaches and this 1930 AEC with Burlingham utility body was listed under the Ashford Belle section of their fleet. The registration originated from Glamorgan. The destination label for Route 27A between Highgate and Richmond Bridge indicates a journey which will finish at Twickenham garage. 'Highgate' was the contemporary term for the terminus we know today as 'Archway Station'. J. F. Higham

As indicated in the table above, no record has been found in official lists of Feltham Transport working from Twickenham garage. However, this Leyland with its Stirling registration is clearly labelled for service on Route 27A between Richmond Bridge and Highgate on 15th January 1949 and so it would seem such operations did happen. The company have also gone to the trouble of putting their name, address and telephone number on the cantrail panels. Alan B. Cross

Upton Park garage (U)

Coaches operated on routes: 15, 40, 101

Operator	Dates
Broadway Coaches (J. Grange & Sons (Plaistow) Ltd)	18th May 1948 to 24th June 1949
Clark's Red Coaches	October 1947 to 22nd July 1949
Clarke's Luxury Coaches	18th May 1948 to 22nd July 1949
Criterion Coaches Ltd	October 1947 to 27th May 1949
Eastern Belle Motor Coaches Ltd	October 1947 to 24th June 1949
Essex County Coaches	7th February 1949 to 27th May 1949
Fallowfield & Britten Ltd	October 1947 to 18th May 1948
Fleet Coaches	21st June 1948 to 8th April 1949
Grey Green Coaches	18th May 1948 to 27th May 1949
Ranelagh Coaches	October 1947 to 24th June 1949
Safeway Coaches	18th May 1948 to 21st June 1948
Thorpe Coaches Ltd	18th May 1948 to 8th April 1949

This 1935 Leyland Tiger of George Ewer's Grey Green Coaches is working from Upton Park garage on the 15. The somewhat severe looking conductor peers at the photographer from the centre entrance. Such a layout must have resulted in very slow loading at busy stops in the West End and City during peak hours.   D. W. K. Jones

A sister vehicle to this Wycombe bodied Gilford Hera is shown elsewhere in this book working for Feltham Transport. Both originated with W. Alexander & Sons and WG 2314 has found its way into the Ranelagh Coaches fleet of C. F. Seyfred of East Ham. Standing at the Ladbroke Grove terminus of Route 15 it is followed by one of Middle Row's early L.G.O.C. STLs.   D. W. K. Jones

Eastern Belle Motor Coaches of Bow Road used this 32-seat Maudslay from Upton Park on Route 15. It previously belonged to Lewis Safety Coaches of Greenwich. On its way through to Ladbroke Grove it pauses at St Clements Danes church in the Strand and the driver looks round to see what is causing the delay. The open site and the buildings behind the coach have actually been rebuilt twice since this picture was taken. The sign on the lamppost directs to Temple Station and Trams, ignoring the nearer Aldwych station, perhaps because the service from there, even in 1948, was patchy to say the least.   D. A. Ruddom collection

A very cheerful East End driver, who could be said to bear some likeness to the popular comedian of the time Arthur Askey, acknowledges the photographer from the cab of his 1938 Leyland TS3. Clark's Red Coaches of Forest Gate were the owners of this smartly turned out vehicle on Route 40. In the background trolleybuses run in and out of the Aldgate Trolleybus and Green Line Coach Station while the bus stop shows the contemporary use of white on black 'E plates' for Sunday routes 9 and 23A.   Alan B. Cross

Ranelagh Coaches of East Ham used four fairly elderly coaches on London Transport services. This AEC Regal, GN9745, dated from 1931. At least the rear entrance of its Hoyle body was compatible with London Transport bus stop positions. The winged logo is rather reminiscent of certain early motoring organisations.   D.W.K.Jones

Uxbridge garage (UX)

Coaches operated on routes: 90A, 223, 225

Operator	Dates
Foster's Luxury Coaches	21st June 1948 to 24th June 1949
Hall Brothers	October 1947 to 19th August 1949

Hired coach operation from Uxbridge garage was not extensive and two of the routes listed could be said to be rather peripheral. The 90A was a peak hour operation worked normally with five STs between Hayes Station and Hayes End and was incorporated into Route 98 after 17th August 1948. The other route, represented in this picture, was the 225 between Eastcote Lane and Northwood Station. Just why Hall Brothers' Maudslay JW4901 – a Wolverhampton registration – is at Hounslow turning into the garage with label in the bulkhead window showing '225 Uxbridge L.T. Garage' is unclear. 'UX 1339' in the top destination box is presumably the telephone and not a duty number. Alan B. Cross

Victoria garage (GM)

Coaches operated on routes: 52, 77, 77A, 137

Operator	Dates
Ansell's Coaches Ltd (S. Ansell & Company, also New Karrymore Coaches Ltd)	23rd October 1947 to 7th February 1949
Orange Coaches (Keith & Boyle) Ltd	23rd October 1947 to 7th February 1949
Red Line Continental Motorways Ltd	Early 1949 to 8th April 1949
Topple's Coaches	June 1948 to 13th October 1948
Winfield's Coaches	24th November 1947 to 8th April 1949

New to North Western Road Car in 1929 this Tilling Stevens B10A was rebodied with a 31-seat Eastern Counties Omnibus Company body in 1935. It now belongs to S. Ansell & Company of Camberwell. On a very wet day in 1947 it stands in the entrance to the basement section of Victoria garage labelled for work on Route 77 from Kings Cross to Tooting.   Alan B. Cross

West Green garage (WG)

Coaches operated on routes: 29, 144

Operator	Dates
Ardley Brothers Ltd	23rd October 1947 to 24th June 1949
Emerald Coaches Ltd	18th May 1948 to 24th June 1949
Frame's Tours Ltd	24th November 1947 to 5th March 1948
Grey Green Coaches	Observation only – not on any official lists
Henry Saloon Coaches Ltd	3rd August 1948 to 27th May 1949
J. M. Motors	18th May 1948 to 13th October 1948
London Road Coaches	3rd August 1948 to 14th February 1949
Monico Motorways	26th January 1948 to 8th April 1949
Viney's Luxury Coaches	October 1947 to 27th May 1949

Working between Victoria and Turnpike Lane on Route 29 this impressive, if elderly, Gilford coach belongs to Emerald Coaches Ltd of Islington. Presumably it is therefore in a green livery. A feature of the 168 OT model was the prominent Gruss air springs mounted here below the headlights. Alan B. Cross

This Blackpool registration, FV 49, would be a cherished registration nowadays for which a large sum might change hands. In 1948, however, it was not regarded as particularly unusual and it graced this Leyland Tiger TS3 of Viney's Luxury Coaches, whose body would appear to be of younger origin than the chassis on which it is mounted. Standing on the far side of the Turnpike Lane bus station it is ready for service on the Victoria to Southgate section of Route 29.   D. W. K. Jones

Three trilby hatted gentlemen, looking rather like the personnel in a London Transport posed photograph of the period, queue up at Victoria to board this Bedford OWB on Route 29 belonging to London Road Coaches of MacKenzie Street, Slough. This may seem a far distant operator to be working from West Green garage but the vehicles used were in fact kept at the Bridge Garage, Green Lanes, Palmers Green which was actually passed on the way to Southgate.   J. F. Higham

Willesden garage (AC)

Coaches operated on routes: 6, 8, 52

Operator	Dates
Clifton and Kalber	23rd October 1947 to 27th May 1949
Progress Coaches (A. E. Fox)	23rd October 1947 to 13th October 1948
Red Line Continental Motorways Ltd	26th January 1948 to 18th May 1948 and
	13th October 1948 to 8th April 1949
Smith's Luxury Coaches	9th August 1948 to 16th November 1948
Valliant Direct Motor Coaches Ltd	October 1947 to 8th April 1949

A 1936 Duple bodied Tilling Stevens belonging to Clifton and Kalber of Craven Park is labelled for operation from Willesden garage on Route 6 between Kensal Rise and Hackney Wick. It is however waiting on the time honoured stand on the offside of the road at Aldwych and so, like the STL behind, is presumably not working the eastern section of the route. The Blackburn registration gives the clue to its original owner which was Lewis Cronshaw Ltd. Capital Transport collection

COUNTRY AREA

Very few official records have been found to still exist regarding the operation of hired coaches in the Country Area. While it was nothing like as widespread as in the Central Area, it did occur. The only 'Roneo' sheet that has come to hand listing Country Area operation is one dated 19th November 1947 which gives the following information.

Chelsham garage (CM)

6 coaches from Graves of Redhill for Route 408 (Warlingham–Epsom) for a 30minute (approx.) supplementary service in weekday peak hours – coaches to be fuelled at Reigate (RG) as no petrol available at either Chelsham (CM) or Godstone (GD).

Leatherhead garage (LH)

3 coaches from Greens of Walton and 1 coach from Bookham Saloons of Bookham for Route 406 (Epsom to Kingston) for weekday peak hour duplication.

Northfleet garage (NF)

1 coach from G. Atkins of Hextable for Route 480 (Dartford to Horns Cross) for peak hour duplication.

Reigate garage (RG)

2 coaches from Graves of Redhill for Routes 405/414 (Redhill to Coulsdon) for a 30minute (approx.) supplementary service in weekday peak hours.

Staines garage (ST)

2 coaches from Graves (*this may be a mistype for Greens)* of Walton for Route 460 (Staines (Bridge Street) to Laleham) for a 30minute (approx.) supplementary service on weekdays. *NOTE: This is a very odd entry since Route 460 never worked from Staines to Laleham, which at the time was exclusively a Central Area stretch of road.*

St Albans garage (SA)

2 coaches from Premier of Watford for Route 330 (St Albans–Hatfield–Welwyn Garden City) for peak hour duplication.

Windsor garage (WR)

1 coach from Try of Windsor (Windsorian) for Route 458 (Slough to Uxbridge) for weekday peak hour duplication. 3 coaches from Try of Windsor (Windsorian) for Route 457 (Windsor to Uxbridge for a 30minute (approx.) supplementary service on weekdays. 4 coaches from Try of Windsor (Windsorian) for Routes 417/441/484 (Langley–Slough–Farnham Road, George) for weekday peak hour duplication. *NOTE: All those services shown as supplementary services were asterisked as 'In anticipation of approved programme of augmentation with new single deck vehicles'.*

Top right Standing in the back yard of St Albans garage on 27th March 1948, Premier Travel GF581 is labelled for service on Route 330 from there to Welwyn Garden City. This coach started life as L.G.O.C. Green Line coach T 64, entering service from Watford, Leavesden Road garage in May 1930 with a Hall Lewis built body. It was sold by London Transport in July 1938 to Horne Products Ltd, a dealer at Colnbrook and from there it was obtained in 1939 by Premier returning to its old home of Watford. They immediately had it rebodied by Thurgoods of Ware and it served them in this condition until October 1953 when it passed on to Barker of Roydon. Alan B. Cross

Centre right This Maudslay of Green Luxury Coaches of Walton-on-Thames has just entered the yard at Kingston Station. It is working as an 'L.P.T.B. Relief', which dates the photograph before the advent of the London Transport Executive on 1st January 1948. With the coach serving the section of 406 between Kingston and Epsom, one is reminded of more recent competitive efforts by certain operators over this section of the route and that it is now a 'red' bus route. Alan B. Cross

Right BKT602, of Bookham Saloons was the sole coach provided by Mr W. A. Freelove for work from Leatherhead garage on the Kingston–Epsom section of Route 406. An AEC Regal with Duple bodywork, it was new to Pilcher of Chatham in June 1935. Standing in the yard at Kingston Station it has a backdrop of Country Area STLs. The photograph is probably post-January 1948 since the sign in window above the rear axle reads 'LONDON TRANSPORT' rather than 'L.P.T.B. RELIEF'. J. F. Higham

This photograph taken opposite Windsor Castle is of Windsorian's Dennis 'Arrow' coach working, presumably from Windsor garage, as a relief on Route 353 (Windsor to Berkhamsted). No official records have been found regarding this operation but obviously it happened and information is still awaited on when exactly and for how long. The coach has a 1931 Berkshire registration and was therefore possibly new to Windsorian, but looks to be in excellent condition. G. F. Ashwell

Coach Companies

Details of companies and vehicles used at one time or another over the period of the scheme.

A and W Omnibus Co. Ltd

A & W Coaches, 40/44 Station Road, North Harrow, Middx

Garage: 331 Pinner Road, Harrow, Middx

Allocated to LT garages: Cricklewood, Edgware, Harrow Weald, Hendon

CPJ	122	Maudslay SF40	35seat Duple *
FXR	336	Leyland Cheetah	32seat Duple *
JMC	271	Albion Valkyrie CX9	33seat Mulliner
LMT	704	Bedford OWB	32seat Duple
MPA	686	Maudslay Marathon III	33seat Dutfield *
MPA	688	Maudslay Marathon	33seat Dutfield *
MPB	891	Maudslay Marathon	33seat Dutfield *
OMT	409	Maudslay Marathon III	33seat Whitson
OMT	410	Maudslay Marathon III	33seat Whitson
OMT	411	Maudslay Marathon III	33seat Whitson
OMT	412	Maudslay Marathon III	33seat Whitson
OMY	465	Maudslay Marathon	33seat Whitson
OMY	583	Maudslay Marathon III	33seat Whitson
OMY	584	Maudslay Marathon III	33seat Whitson
OMY	585	Maudslay Marathon	33seat Whitson
SMF	338	Maudslay Marathon III	33seat Whitson
SMF	339	Maudslay Marathon III	33seat Westnor
TMV	115	Maudslay Marathon III	33seat Whitson
TMV	116	Maudslay Marathon III	33seat Whitson
TMV	262	Maudslay Marathon III	33seat Whitson
TMV	311	Maudslay Marathon III	33seat Whitson

* On loan from P. Crouch, Guildford

Ace Coaches

see Futcher, G. J.

Acorn Motors Ltd

Hanworth Coaches, 24 Cross Road, Hanworth, Middx

Garage: At address above

Allocated to LT garages: Hounslow, Kingston

FJ	9061	Dennis Lancet	31seat Duple
KX	8092	Dennis Lancet	32seat Duple
AKL	472	Dennis Lancet	31seat Duple
EPA	161	Bedford WTB	25seat Body not confirmed
LMX	111	Dennis Lancet	32seat Dennis
LMY	645	Dennis Lancet	34seat Body not confirmed
LMY	646	Bedford WTB	25seat Body not confirmed

Adnams, L.

see United Service Transport Co. Ltd.

Advance Motor Services
A. Clark & Sons, 85 Forest Drive East, Leytonstone, E11

Garage: Broadway Garage, 9 The Broadway, Highams Park

Allocated to LT garage: Leyton

| DGK | 673 | Leyland Cub | 26seat Duple |
| DYK | 327 | Leyland Cub | 27seat Duple |

Alexandra Coaches
H. A. Clarke, Enfield, Middx

One coach from this operator noted at Chiswick in March 1948 but no record found of operation.

| JX | 5395 | Leyland Cheetah |

Ansell's Coaches
S. Ansell & Co., (New Karrymore Coaches Ltd)
220 Camberwell Road, Camberwell, SE5

Garages: Rust Square, Camberwell, SE5
                   35A Naylor Road, Peckham, SE15

Allocated to LT garages: Camberwell, Hackney, Nunhead, Victoria.

CS	3356	Leyland Cheetah	35seat Alexander
CS	3359	Leyland Cheetah	37seat Alexander
CS	3375	Leyland Cheetah	37seat Alexander
DB	5234	Tilling Stevens B10A2	31seat E.C.O.C.
FV	972	Tilling Stevens B10A2	36seat Burlingham
GW	649	Leyland Tiger TS4	32seat Harrington
HD	3440	Leyland Tiger TS1	31seat Weymann
VT	7140	Tilling Stevens B10A2	32seat Lauton
XS	4765	Albion Valkyrie 3axle	39seat Cowieson
YS	4488	Albion Valkyrie PW69	35seat Cowieson
CLA	933	Maudslay ML5	35seat Duple
CUC	770	Maudslay ML5	32seat Duple
HUW	164	Bedford OB	26seat Duple
HXY	508	Maudslay Marathon II	35seat Duple

Ardley Brothers Ltd
Windsor Park Garage, Dowsett Road, Tottenham, N17

Garage: At address above

Allocated to LT garages: Tottenham, West Green.

OMT	602	Bedford OB	29seat Duple
OMY	410	Bedford OB	29seat Duple
OMY	520	Bedford OB	29seat Duple
SMF	8	Bedford OB	27seat Duple
SMF	585	Bedford OB	27seat Duple

Argosy Super Coaches
F. W. B. Smith, Coach Station, Canal Head, Peckham, SE15

Garage: At address above

Allocated to LT garages: Battersea, Nunhead, Streatham

GV	411	Leyland Tiger TS	32seat Petty
JA	8865	Bedford WTB	25seat *Body not confirmed*
TE	5711	Leyland Tiger TS2	32seat Leyland
FDA	257	Leyland PS1	33seat Mulliner
HYN	466	Leyland PS1	33seat Harrington

Ashford Belle
see Roberts & Dickenson

Atkins, Fred G.
The Garage, Hextable, Swanley, Kent
Garage: Crisp Bros, High Street, Sidcup, Kent
Allocated to LT garages: Northfleet, Sidcup.

GN	1368	AEC Regal	33seat Harrington
GN	1376	AEC Regal	32seat Harrington
CLY	18	Leyland Tiger TS7	33seat Harrington

Avondale Safety Coaches
Tatnall Brothers Ltd, 116 Becontree Avenue, Dagenham, Essex
Garage: At address above
Allocated to LT garage: Seven Kings.

UR	9535	AEC Regal	32seat Petty
AYE	388	AEC Regal	32seat Strachan
DXF	587	Dennis Lancet II	32seat Strachan

Avonley Coaches
P. F. McCafferty, 1/2A Briant Street, Deptford, SE14
Garage: 204 Hither Green Lane, Lewisham, SE13
Allocated to LT garage: Catford.

XS	4407	Albion Valkyrie 3 axle	39seat Cowieson
XS	5110	Albion Valkyrie CX11	35seat Cowieson
FTT	807	Bedford OWB	28seat Duple *(utility)*
GAL	596	Bedford OWB	32seat Duple *(utility)*

Banfield, Charles W.
326 Walworth Road, SE17
Garage: 7A Coopers Road, Old Kent Road, SE15
Allocated to LT garages: Camberwell, Nunhead, Old Kent Road.

CK	4746	Leyland Tiger TS6	35seat English Electric
EV	1266	Leyland Tiger TS4	32seat London Lorries
KJ	2376	Leyland Tiger TS2	32seat Short
KJ	5432	Leyland Tiger TS3	32seat Short
KJ	5440	Leyland Tiger TS4	32seat Short
SC	4374	Leyland Tiger TS2	32seat Duple
SC	4376	Leyland Tiger TS2	32seat Duple
CBA	765	Leyland PS1	33seat Burlingham
DGG	892	Bedford OWB	28seat Duple
FGT	950	Leyland Tiger TS2	32seat Duple
FLE	509	Bedford WTB	26seat Duple
FUU	968	Bedford WTB	26seat Duple
HTC	283	Leyland PS1	32seat Plaxton
HUC	273	Leyland Lion LT5	32seat Weymann
HYN	467	Bedford OB	29seat Duple
JXH	163	Bedford OB	29seat Duple
JXL	451	Leyland PS1	32seat Strachan
JXL	452	Leyland PS1	32seat Strachan
JXL	478	Bedford OB	29seat Duple
TMV	502	Bedford OB	29seat Duple

Barking Coaches Ltd
Library Garage, Ripple Way, Barking, Essex

Garage: Coverdale Road, Barking, Essex

Allocated to LT garage: Barking.

ETW 89	Ford (FC)	26seat Mulliner *(utility)* *
KRF 853	Dennis Lancet	38seat *Body not confirmed*
SML 467	Bedford OB	29seat Duple †

* *Formerly ran for T. W. Halpin (q.v.)*
† *Formerly ran for Lacey's (East Ham) Ltd (q.v.)*

Battens Coaches Ltd
451/3 Barking Road, East Ham, E6

Garage: At address above

Allocated to LT garage: Barking.

HV 2751	AEC Regal	32seat Park Royal *
HV 2752	AEC Regal	35seat Park Royal
HV 2753	AEC Regal	32seat Park Royal
AJD 538	Bedford OWB	29seat Duple
CHM 132	AEC Regal	35seat Thurgood
CHV 518	Daimler CVD6	35seat Thurgood

* *Sold to Bontonian 3/48 (q.v.)*

Bennett, A and Sons
see Shirley Coaches

Bennett, John (Croydon) Ltd
23 London Road, Croydon, Surrey

Garage: Peall Road, Thornton Road, Croydon, Surrey

Allocated to LT garages: Elmers End, Streatham, Sutton.

OY 2568	Leyland Tiger TS4	33seat Harrington
OY 2569	Leyland Tiger TS4	32seat Harrington
OY 2570	Leyland Tiger TS4	33seat Harrington
OY 2574	Leyland Tiger TS4	32seat Harrington
OY 2577	Leyland Tiger TS4	32seat Harrington
GBY 85	Bedford OB	29seat Duple
GBY 567	Bedford OB	29seat Duple
GBY 800	Bedford OB	29seat Duple

Bexleyheath Transport Co. Ltd
R. Margo *see also under Margo's – some confusion as to ownership of some vehicles.*
57A The Broadway, Bexleyheath, Kent

Garage: Pincott Road, Bexleyheath, Kent

Allocated to LT garage: Sidcup.

GN 1378	AEC Regal	32seat Harrington
JG 1442	Tilling Stevens B49CZ	35seat Hoyal
ARK 568	Dennis Lancet	32seat Harrington
CNN 865	Leyland Lion LT7	39seat Duple
DKK 677	Dennis Lancet II	32seat Duple
EKK 107	Dennis Lancet II	32seat Duple

Bickley Coaches
Southlands Road, Bickley, Kent

Garage:	At address above	
Allocated to LT garage:	Bromley.	
ANO 345	Tilling Stevens	32seat Duple *(utility)*

Bingley Bros Ltd
see Sceptre Coaches

Black & White Coaches Ltd
Davis Luxury Coach, Selborne Road, Walthamstow, E17

Garage:	210 Hoe Street, Walthamstow, E17	
Allocated to LT garage:	Tottenham.	
GF 5249	AEC Regal	32seat Beadle
GH 3828	AEC Regal (ex-T 222)	32seat Ransomes*
ABH 307	AEC Regal	32seat Strachan
AGH 297	Leyland Tiger TS4	32seat Harrington
AGH 298	Leyland Tiger TS4	32seat Harrington
CNO 30	Tilling Stevens	31seat Duple
DAU 453	AEC Regal	32seat Craven
MEV 321	Bedford OB	28seat Black & White

* May have been rebodied.

Blue & White Star Transport Co. Ltd
White Star Transport, 4 Surbiton Crescent, Kingston, Surrey

Garage:	Southsea Road, Kingston, Surrey	
Allocated to LT garage:	Kingston.	
JPK 498	Bedford OWB	32seat Duple *(utility)*
JPK 871	Bedford OWB	32seat Duple *(utility)*
JPK 872	Bedford OWB	32seat Duple *(utility)*

Blue Belle Motors Ltd
see United Service Transport Co. Ltd

Bontonian Coaches
H. Charik, 19 Charlbury Gardens, Seven Kings, Essex

Garage:	Barking Motor Company, Ilford Lane, Ilford, Essex	
Allocated to LT garage:	Seven Kings.	
HV 2751	AEC Regal	32seat Park Royal *
PG 7025	AEC Regal	32seat Strachan

* Formerly ran for Battens Coaches (q.v.)

Bookham Saloons
W. A. Freelove, Leatherhead, Surrey

Garage:	At address above	
Allocated to LT garage:	Leatherhead.	
BKT 602	AEC Regal	32seat Duple

Boughton's Coaches Ltd
Boughton's Service Station Ltd
17/31 Chilton Street, Bethnal Green, E2

Garage: At address above

Allocated to LT garage: Dalston.

ADL	539	Dennis Lancet	33seat *Body not confirmed*
BRE	338	Dennis Lancet	32seat *Body not confirmed*
CAW	885	Bedford OWB	28seat Duple
ETW	862	Bedford WTB	25seat Duple
ETW	863	Bedford WTB	25seat Metcalfe
HVW	706	Bodford OLD	25seat *Body not confirmed* *
KGN	924	Bedford OB	30seat Plaxton
KGT	424	Bedford OB	30seat Plaxton

* This registration is recorded as being a new lorry pre-war.

Bourne & Balmer (Croydon) Ltd
97 George Street, Croydon, Surrey

Garage: Coach Station, Dingwall Road, Croydon, Surrey

Allocated to LT garage: Croydon.

CRK	441	Dennis Lancet II	32seat Harrington
DRK	51	Dennis Lancet II	32seat Harrington
DRK	52	Dennis Lancet II	32seat Harrington
EOY	337	AEC Regal	32seat Harrington
GBY	128	AEC Regal I	32seat Harrington
GBY	640	AEC Regal I	32seat Harrington
GRK	399	AEC Regal I	32seat Harrington
GRK	737	AEC Regal I	33seat Harrington

Bowler, A. E.
see Hampton Coaches

Bradshaw's Super Coaches Ltd
14 Lakedale Road, Woolwich, SE18

Garage: Bradshaw's Garage, Ceres Road, Woolwich, SE18

Allocated to LT garages: Athol Street, Plumstead.

HUU	852	AEC Regal I	32seat Duple
HUU	853	AEC Regal I	33seat Duple
HXB	457	AEC Regal I	33seat Duple
HXB	458	AEC Regal I	33seat Duple
HXB	459	AEC Regal I	33seat Duple
HXX	632	Bedford OB	29seat Duple
HYE	297	Bedford OB	29seat Duple
HYE	300	Bedford OB	29seat Duple
HYM	187	AEC Regal I	32seat Harrington
HYN	420	Bedford OB	29seat Duple
HYO	300	AEC Regal I	32seat Harrington
HYO	981	Bedford OB	29seat Duple
HYO	985	Bedford OB	29seat Duple
HYO	988	Bedford OB	29seat Duple
JLM	501	AEC Regal	33seat Harrington
JUV	297	Bedford OB	29seat Duple
JXM	763	Daimler CVD6	33seat Harrington

Broadway Coaches
J. Grange & Sons (Plaistow) Ltd, 589 Barking Road, East Ham, E6

Garage: 448/454 Barking Road, East Ham, E6

Allocated to LT garages: Barking, Upton Park.

GF	597	AEC Regal (ex-T 86)	32seat Wadham *(rebodied since LT days)*
JG	5448	Leyland Tiger TS7	32seat Park Royal
ARR	829	AEC 'Q'	32seat Cravens
CHM	708	Dennis Lancet III	35seat Duple
LMH	955	Leyland Tiger TS4	32seat Duple

Broadway Coaches (J. Hanslip)
see Crouch End Luxury

Brooks & Palmer
see Ferndale Coaches

Burfoot and Jones
see Star Luxury Coaches

Butler, W. F.
see Sydenham Coaches

Camden Coaches Ltd
43 Glengall Road, Edgware, Middx

Garage: Flight's Garage, Parkhurst Road, Holloway, N7

Allocated to LT garages: Chalk Farm, Holloway.

DY	8062	AEC Regal	32seat Harrington
DYF	770	Dennis Lancet II	32seat Metcalfe
HYF	906	Bedford OWB	29seat Duple
HYK	367	Morris	29seat *Body not confirmed*
HYK	836	Bedford OB	29seat Duple
HYR	257	Bedford OB	29seat Duple
KGH	310	Bedford OB	29seat Duple

Careford's Coaches
C. H. T. Careford
439 Hertford Road, Enfield, Middx

Garage: At address above

Allocated to LT garage: Enfield.

| CK | 4728 | Leyland Tiger TS6 | 31seat Leyland |
| WG | 4547 | Bedford WTB | ? seat *Body not confirmed* |

Carshalton & Wallington Coaches Ltd
G. Lambird
173 Stafford Road, Wallington, Surrey

Garage: At address above

Allocated to LT garage: Sutton.

ALM	266	AEC Regal	32seat Duple
DHR	24	Bedford OWB	28seat Duple
JXH	555	Bedford OB	29seat Duple
LMG	484	Bedford OWB	28seat Duple

Carter's
W. J. Carter
341 Camden Road, Holloway, N7

Garage: Flight's Garage, Parkhurst Road, Holloway, N7

Allocated to LT garage: Holloway.

| XS | 2823 | Albion Viking | 32seat Duple |
| BXO | 209 | AEC Regal | 32seat Harrington |

Castle Coaches
C. C. Grundon
117 Mount Pleasant Road, Lewisham, SE13

Garage: 204 Hither Green Lane, Lewisham, SE13

Allocated to LT garages: Bromley, Catford, Norwood.

UU	9342	AEC Reliance	32seat Beadle
WS	8020	Leyland Cheetah LZ2	36seat Alexander
DYL	904	Leyland FEC (ex-TF 1)	34seat Leyland
KRF	106	Bedford OWB	28seat Mulliner
KRF	111	Bedford OWB	28seat Mulliner
KRF	114	Bedford OWB	29seat Mulliner

Champion Coaches
C. A. Champion
232 Hall Lane, Chingford, E4 (later 31 Grove Road, Chingford, E4)

Garage: At address above

Allocated to LT garages: Enfield, Tottenham.

GW	2008	Gilford 168OT	32seat Wycombe
PG	9575	Gilford 168OT	33seat Metcalfe
MVW	15	Maudslay Marathon II	33seat Whitson
NTW	140	Crossley SD42/7	33seat Whitson

Charik, H.
see Bontonian Coaches

Cheek, H.
see Elms Coaches

Clark, A. & Sons
see Advance Motor Services

Clarke, H. A.
see Alexandra Coaches

Clark's Red Coaches
F. E. V. Clark
248 Romford Road, Forest Gate, E7

Garage: At address above

Allocated to LT garages: Forest Gate, Upton Park.

CS	112	Gilford Hera 176SD	32seat Wycombe
UF	5807	Leyland Tiger TS2	32seat Park Royal
BJD	815	Bedford OB	29seat Duple
BXV	335	Leyland Titan TD1	32seat *Body not confirmed* *

CAN	155	Bedford OB	29seat Duple
CAN	260	Bedford OB	29seat Duple
EOC	347	Leyland Tiger TS3	31seat Plaxton
EYE	598	Leyland Tiger TS2	32seat Duple
FOR	169	Leyland PS1	33seat Duple

* Single deck coach body

Clarke's Luxury Coaches
17 Beckton Road, Canning Town, E16

Garage: At address above

Allocated to LT garages: Athol Street, Barking, Forest Gate, Upton Park.

JD	9253	AEC Regal	33seat Strachan
KX	8644	AEC Regal (ex-T 366)	33seat Duple *†
HYN	488	AEC Regal	35seat Duple
HYN	490	Dennis Lancet III	35seat Duple
JXC	778	Dennis Lancet III	35seat Duple
JXD	650	Bedford OB	29seat Duple
JXT	527	AEC Regal III	33seat Duple
KGT	18	Dennis Lancet III	35seat Duple
KYC	326	Crossley SD42/3	33seat Windover
KYC	327	Crossley SD42/3	33seat Windover

† Rebodied May 1939
* Later ran with Overland Lismore Coaches (q.v.)

Classique Coaches Ltd
479 Lea Bridge Road, Leyton, E10

Garage: At address above

Allocated to LT garage: Leyton.

EV	423	Maudslay ML3E	32seat London Lorries ?
EV	424	Maudslay ML3E	32seat London Lorries ?
EV	942	Maudslay ML3E	32seat London Lorries ?
EV	943	Maudslay ML3E	32seat London Lorries ?
BXK	78	Bedford WTL	26seat Duple
GVW	313	Bedford WTB	26seat Duple
LHK	913	Maudslay Marathon II	33seat Duple
LNO	91	Maudslay Marathon II	33seat Duple
LNO	298	Maudslay Marathon II	33seat Duple
LNO	299	Maudslay Marathon II	33seat Duple
MPU	400	Maudslay Marathon II	35seat Duple

Cliff's Saloon Coaches Ltd
142A Well Hall Road, Eltham, SE9

Garage: 48 Foots Cray Road, Eltham, SE9

Allocated to LT garage: Bromley.

EYE	594	Leyland Titan TD1	32seat Duple *
EYE	595	Leyland Titan TD1	32seat Duple *
HXW	113	Bedford OB	29seat Duple
HXX	828	Bedford OB	29seat Duple
HYN	688	Bedford OB	29seat Duple
HYO	990	Bedford OB	29seat Duple
JXH	545	Bedford OB	29seat Duple
JXP	453	Bedford OB	29seat Duple

* Single deck coach body

Clifton & Kalber
81 Clitterhouse Crescent, Cricklewood, NW2

Garage: 79 Craven Park Road, Willesden, NW10

Allocated to LT garages: Shepherds Bush, Willesden.

BV	5740	Tilling Stevens	32seat Duple
WN	9380	Dennis Lancet	32seat Andrews *
FMP	979	Leyland Lion LT7	35seat Duple

* *Formerly ran for Dryer's Coaches (q.v.)*

Cosy Coaches
R. E. Nealon
12 Cherry Orchard, Staines, Middx

Garage: Garner's 174A High Street, Hounslow, Middx

Allocated to LT garage: Turnham Green.

JF	2779	Dennis Lancet 1	32seat *Duple*
UU	9161	AEC Regent	32seat *Body not confirmed* *
DUS	486	Bedford OWB	28seat Duple *(utility)*
DUU	715	Leyland Lion LT7	35seat *Body not confirmed*
TMV	18	Austin CXB	29seat Allweather

* *This coach had a Leyland radiator and a single deck coach body.*

Couch, W.
see Cream Coaches Ltd

County Coaches
see Twigg, S. V.

Cowell, W.
371 New North Road, Islington, N1

Garages: 123 Shepperton Road, Islington, N1
                          Flight's Garage, Parkhurst Road, Holloway, N7

Allocated to LT garages: Chalk Farm, Holloway.

NV	3778	Maudslay ML3	32seat Spite
VX	7851	Gilford 168SD	26seat Duple

Cream Coaches Ltd
W. Couch
474 Andre Street, Hackney, E8

Garage: At address above

Allocated to LT garage: Clayhall.

GGC	770	Bedford OWB	32seat Duple
GGC	771	Bedford OWB	32seat Duple
GLH	203	Bedford OWB	32seat Mulliner
GLH	204	Bedford OWB	32seat Mulliner

Criterion Coaches Ltd
I. Jacobs
166 Wanstead Park Avenue, Manor Park, E12

Garage: Aldersbrook Garage, Aldersbrook Road, Manor Park, E12

Allocated to LT garage: Upton Park.

OML	915	Bedford OB	28seat Duple

Cronshaw, Lewis Ltd
94 Brent Street, Hendon, NW4

Garage: At address above

Allocated to LT garages: Chalk Farm, Cricklewood, Hendon, Holloway.

BV	4454	Leyland Tiger TS7	32seat Duple
BV	7038	Leyland Tiger TS7	32seat Duple
BBV	418	Daimler CVD6	35seat Duple
BBV	419	Daimler CVD6	35seat Duple
BBV	622	Dennis Lancet III	35seat Duple
BBV	623	Dennis Lancet III	35seat Duple
BBV	656	Daimler CVD6	35seat Duple
BCB	7	Bedford OB	29seat Duple
BCB	143	Daimler CVD6	35seat Duple
BCB	477	Dennis Lancet III	35seat Duple
BCB	684	Bedford OB	29seat Duple
OML	825	Bedford OB	29seat Duple

Crouch End Luxury
Broadway Coaches, J. Hanslip, 39 Topsfield Parade, Hornsey, N8

Garages: Capitol Motor Garage, Tottenham Lane, Hornsey, N8 – 24/11/47
Priory Road, Hornsey, N8 (5/48)

Allocated to LT garage: Muswell Hill.

MMP	169	Bedford OB	29seat Duple
MMP	170	Bedford OB	29seat Duple
MMP	171	AEC Regal	35seat Duple
SMY	248	AEC Regal III	35seat Duple

Cumfilery Coaches
see Wright Bros (London) Ltd

Currie, P. Ltd
Dewlands Farm, Stone, Dartford, Kent

Garage: 184/190 Blackfen Road, Sidcup, Kent

Allocated to LT garage: Sidcup.

| BCJ | 620 | Bedford WTB | 26seat Duple |
| DTO | 15 | Leyland Cub | 25seat Duple |

Curtis & Hearn
Angel Garage, Milespit Hill, Mill Hill, NW7

Garage: At address above

Allocated to LT garages: Cricklewood, Edgware, Hendon.

| BV | 5741 | Tilling Stevens | 32seat Duple |
| TMV | 8 | Bedford OB | 29seat Duple |

D & R Motor Company
D & R Motor Coaches, W. Davey, 25 Cowley Road, Lambeth, SW9

Garage: S. Ansell & Company, 15A Rust Square, Camberwell, SE5

Allocated to LT garage: Camberwell.

AG	6212	Tilling Stevens B10C2	31seat Burlingham
AG	6216	Tilling Stevens B10A2	31seat Brush
DR	4785	Leyland Lion PLSC	33seat Mumford

Dacosta, J & H
see Gatehouse Coaches

Dagenham Coach Services
67 Hunters Hall Road, Dagenham, Essex

Garage:　　　　Grays Farm, Church Elm Lane, Dagenham, Essex

Allocated to LT garages: Barking, Hornchurch, Seven Kings.

DPD	859	Dennis Ace	20seat Dennis
LNO	414	Albion PW67	32seat Cowieson ?

Davis, Fred & Sons
Roseland, 337 Westbourne Park Road, Paddington, W11

Garage:　　　　9 Roseland Place, Portobello Road, North Kensington, W11

Allocated to LT garage: Middle Row.

AUP	429	Dennis Lancet II	32seat *Body not confirmed*
BLO	901	Gilford Hera 176S	32seat Wycombe
HYE	184	Commer Commando	30seat Plaxton

Davis, L. C. & Sons
1 The Bungalows, Streatham Road, Mitcham, SW16

Garage:　　　　　　At address above

Allocated to LT garages: Battersea, Elmers End, Hammersmith, Merton, Mortlake, Putney Bridge, Streatham.

GH	3802	AEC Regal (ex-T 228)	32seat Ransomes
WH	8650	AEC Regal	32seat Watson
WN	4869	AEC Regent	32seat Harrington *
DPU	90	AEC Regal	32seat Duple
KPG	997	AEC Regal	32seat Duple
LML	157	Bedford OWB	32seat Duple
LMT	613	Bedford OWB	32seat Duple
LMV	387	AEC Regal (ex-T324†)	32seat Duple
LPF	876	AEC Regal	32seat Dutfield
LPL	800	AEC Regal	33seat King & Taylor
MME	742	Bedford OB	29seat Duple
MME	743	Bedford OB	29seat Duple
MME	744	Bedford OB	29seat Duple
MME	745	Bedford OB	29seat Duple
TMG	724	Leyland PS1/1	33seat Dutfield
TMV	994	Leyland PS1/1	33seat Duple

* *Single deck coach body*
† *Re-registered, was PL 6476*

Davis Luxury Coach
see Black and White Coaches Ltd

Dawson
? Walthamstow

Garage:　　　　　　Probably at Walthamstow

Allocated to LT garage: Tottenham.

This operator appears on one early LT list but no other details have been traced. It may have been a clerical error for Davis (Black and White Coaches Ltd) of Walthamstow.

Dix Luxury Coaches
J. Wordsworth, Heath Garage, Wood Lane, Dagenham, Essex

Garage: At address above

Allocated to LT garages: Barking, Seven Kings.

MHK	548	Guy Arab III	33seat Strachan
MHK	549	Guy Arab III	33seat Strachan
MTW	985	Maudslay Marathon	33seat Whitson *
MVW	725	Austin CKB	29seat Mann Egerton
MVX	376	Bedford OB	29seat Duple
MVX	881	Maudslay Marathon II	35seat Whitson *
NEV	190	Bedford OB	29seat Whitson
NNO	229	Bedford OB	29seat Strachan
NTW	706	Bedford OB	29seat Duple

* *Sold to Universal Coaches November 1948 (q.v.)*

Down, A. P.
44A/46 Langley Avenue, Worcester Park, Surrey

Garage: Langley Garage, 118 London Road, North Cheam, Surrey

Allocated to LT garage: Sutton.

HYN	699	Bedford OB	29seat Duple

Downey, J.
see Fleet Coaches

Downey, J. J. & B. R.
Escort Coaches, 2A Ranelagh Road, East Ham, E6

Garage: At address above

Allocated to LT garage: Forest Gate.

ERF	308	Dennis Lancet II	32seat Dennis

Dryer's Coaches Ltd
G. Dryer, 197 Wadham Road, Walthamstow, E17

Garage: Flight's Garage, Parkhurst Road, Holloway, N7

Allocated to LT garages: Hackney, Holloway.

WN	9380	Dennis Lancet II	32seat Andrews *
JXT	614	Bedford OB	29seat Woodall Nicholson
MVW	155	Bedford OB	29seat Duple

* *Sold to Clifton & Kalber 5/48 (q.v.)*

Eastern Belle Motor Coaches Ltd
167A Bow Road, Bow, E3

Garage: At address above

Allocated to LT garages: Athol Street, Hackney, Upton Park.

WJ	6505	Leyland Tiger TS4	32seat Cravens
AYH	93	Maudslay ML3	32seat Duple
BPX	733	Bedford WTB	25seat Duple
HGK	798	AEC Regal III	35seat Duple
HLH	305	Leyland Tiger TS4	31seat Harrington
HXW	746	AEC Regal	33seat Plaxton
JXH	768	AEC Regal	33seat Plaxton

Ellis, B.
see Ideal Safety Coaches

Elms Coaches
H. Cheek, 384 Kenton Road, Kenton, Middx
Garage: At address above
Allocated to LT garage: Hendon.

JT	4745	Commer	25seat *Body not confirmed*

Elms, Longman Motor Services Ltd
Edwin Longman Ltd *See also Harrison & Hole.*
41 Ardfillan Road, Catford, SE6
Garage: 643 Old Kent Road, Peckham, SE15
Allocated to LT garages: Camberwell, Old Kent Road.

DB	9487	Leyland Tiger TS4	33seat Harrington
GF	595	AEC Regal (ex-T 127)	32seat *Body not confirmed (rebodied)*
GN	9571	AEC Regal	33seat Hoyal
HV	1184	Tilling Stevens	32seat Beadle
CUW	334	Dennis Ace	24seat Dennis
MPB	894	Crossley SD42	33seat Dutfield

Elms, Phillips & Brown
599 High Road, Tottenham, N17
Garage: At address above
Allocated to LT garages: Palmers Green, Tottenham.

WG	1276	Gilford 168OT	32seat Wycombe
LMG	475	Bedford OWB	28seat Duple
OML	312	Bedford OB	29seat Duple
OMY	378	Bedford OB	29seat Duple

Emerald Coaches Ltd
W. King & Sons Ltd, 123a Shepperton Road, Islington, N1
Garage: At address above
Allocated to LT garages: Hackney, West Green.

GK	8612	Gilford 168OT	28seat Abbott
CVH	317	Bedford OB	29seat Roberts (Huddersfield)
DEL	102	Bedford WTB	25seat Duple
FDH	430	Leyland Cub	26seat Burlingham
HGF	323	Bedford OB	32seat Duple
HYP	220	Dennis Lancet III	35seat Duple
MPU	61	Bedford OB	29seat Black & White
MPU	62	Bedford OB	29seat Black & White
NRF	301	Bedford OB	26seat Burlingham
SML	474	Daimler CVD6	33seat Yorkshire Yacht Co.
SML	475	Daimler CVD6	33seat Yorkshire Yacht Co.

Empress Coaches
J. G. Green
169 Fulham Palace Road, Hammersmith, W6, later 57 Petley Road, Hammersmith, W6
Garage: Laundry Road, Hammersmith, W6
Allocated to LT garages: Hammersmith, Mortlake, Putney Bridge.

DF	8186	Leyland Tiger TS2	32seat London Lorries
WN	4370	Leyland Tiger TS4	32seat Harrington or Beadle ?
CXW	364	Dennis Lancet II	32seat Duple
JUV	352	Dennis Lancet III	33seat Duple
MMY	680	Bedford OB	27seat Duple

Empress Motors Ltd
2 Corbridge Crescent, Bethnal Green, E2
Garage: At address above
Allocated to LT garages: Clayhall, Dalston, Hackney.

EN	6580	Dennis Lancet II	32seat Dennis
AXO	518	Dennis Lancet	29seat Duple
DLY	984	Dennis Lancet II	33seat Duple
EXO	529	Morris Dictator	33seat Duple
EXO	530	Morris Dictator	33seat Duple
HYK	993	Bedford OB	29seat Duple *
HYO	705	Dennis Lancet III	35seat Duple
HYO	706	Bedford OB	29seat Duple
HYP	559	Bedford OB	29seat Duple *
HYU	786	Bedford OB	29seat Duple
JXF	327	Bedford OB	29seat Duple
JXL	376	Bedford OB	29seat Duple
JXL	377	Dennis Lancet III	35seat Duple

* *On loan from Fallowfield & Britten*

Enterprise Coaches
A. W. Latham, 26 Farrer Road, Kenton, Middx
Garage: 333 Pinner Road, North Harrow, Middx
Allocated to LT garages: Harrow Weald, Hendon.

KJ	1968	AEC Regal	33seat Santus
VH	7535	AEC Regal	32seat Park Royal
OMT	367	Maudslay Marathon III	33seat Strachan

Escort Coaches
see Downey, J. J & B. R.

Essex County Coaches
219 Lea Bridge Road, Leyton, E10
Garage: At address above
Allocated to LT garages: Leyton, Tottenham, Upton Park.

LMY	449	Bedford OB	29seat Duple
LMY	450	Bedford OB	29seat Duple
LMY	682	Bedford OB	29seat Duple
MMP	813	Bedford OB	28seat Duple

Ewer, George & Co. Ltd
see Grey Green Coaches

Fairway, The
see Pearl and Gunn

Fallowfield & Britten Ltd
23 Mare Street, Hackney, E8

| *Garages:* | 164 Mare Street, Hackney, E8. |
| | 387 Bethnal Green Road, Bethnal Green, E2 |

Allocated to LT garages: Athol Street, Dalston, Holloway, Tottenham, Upton Park.

HYK	991	Bedford OB	29seat Duple
HYK	992	Bedford OB	29seat Duple
HYK	993	Bedford OB	29seat Duple *
HYM	685	Bedford OB	29seat Duple
HYN	479	Bedford OB	29seat Duple
HYN	480	Bedford OB	29seat Duple
HYO	495	Bedford OB	29seat Duple
HYP	559	Bedford OB	29seat Duple *
MMT	875	Bedford OB	29seat Duple
MMT	877	Bedford OB	29seat Duple

* *also ran on hire to Empress Motors Ltd (q.v.)*

Feltham Transport Co.
537 Staines Road, Bedfont, Middx

Garage: At address above

Allocated to LT garage: Hounslow.

MS	8666	Leyland Tiger TS1	32seat Alexander
MS	8828	Leyland Tiger TS1	32seat Alexander
MS	8834	Leyland Tiger TS1	32seat Alexander
WG	2310	Gilford Hera L176S	32seat Wycombe

Ferndale Coaches
Brooks & Palmer, 32 Rancliffe Road, East Ham, E6

Garage: North Woolwich Garage, Albert Road, North Woolwich, E16

Allocated to LT garage: Forest Gate.

DPU	648	Bedford WTB	26seat Duple
DUU	713	Leyland Tiger TS7	32seat Duple
HYN	462	Leyland PS1/1	35seat Duple
LME	673	AEC Regal	33seat Duple
SML	400	Bedford OB	29seat Duple

Fleet Coaches
J. Downey
59–69 Silvertown Way, Canning Town, E16

Garage: At address above

Allocated to LT garage: Upton Park.

| GO | 1044 | Leyland Tiger TS1 | 32seat *Body not confirmed* |

Foster's Luxury Coaches
J. Foster, 73 Cowley Road, Uxbridge, Middx

Garage: Wiseley's Garage, Tavistock Road, Yiewsley, Middx

Allocated to LT garage: Uxbridge.

| CMO | 498 | Bedford OWB | 28seat Mulliner |

Fox, A. E.
see Progress Coaches

Frame's Tours Ltd
80 Southampton Row, WC1

Garage: Flight's Garage, Parkhurst Road, Holloway, N7

Allocated to LT garages: Holloway, West Green.

HYO	197	Bedford OB	27seat Duple
HYP	847	Bedford OB	27seat Duple

Freelove, W. A.
see Bookham Saloons

Freemantle & Dobson
see Progress Coaches

Futcher, G. J.
Ace Coaches
4 Ace Parade, Hook, Surrey

Garage: Bentall's Garage, Kingston upon Thames, Surrey

Allocated to LT garage: Kingston.

JXL	60	Bedford OB	29seat Duple

Garner's Coaches Ltd
Garner, T. E. Hounslow Star, 39 South Ealing Road, Ealing, W5

Garage: 174A High Street, Hounslow, Middx

Allocated to LT garages: Hounslow, Putney Bridge, Turnham Green, Twickenham.

AJW	871	AEC Regal	32seat Strachan
DXF	582	Dennis Lancet II	32seat Strachan
DXF	583	Dennis Lancet II	32seat Strachan
DXF	584	Dennis Lancet II	32seat Strachan
DXF	585	Dennis Lancet II	32seat Strachan
DXF	586	Dennis Lancet II	32seat Strachan
DYF	751	Bedford WTB	29seat Duple
JMC	994	Dennis Lancet II	35seat Duple
LMY	254	Bedford OB	27seat Duple
LMY	462	Bedford OB	27seat Duple
MMT	506	Bedford OB	29seat Duple
MMT	507	Bedford OB	29seat Duple
MMT	508	Bedford OB	29seat Duple
MMT	861	Bedford OB	27seat Duple
MMT	862	Bedford OB	27seat Duple
MMT	863	Bedford OB	27seat Duple
MMT	864	Bedford OB	27seat Duple
MMT	865	Bedford OB	27seat Duple
MMT	866	Bedford OB	27seat Duple
OMY	385	Bedford OB	29seat Duple
OMY	386	Bedford OB	29seat Duple
SME	314	Dennis Lancet III	35seat Duple

Gatehouse Coaches
J & H Dacosta
36 Tollington Road, Holloway, N7
Garage: Flight's Garage, Parkhurst Road, Holloway, N7
Allocated to LT garage: Holloway.

| CEL | 326 | Bedford WTB | 25seat Duple |
| JNK | 500 | Dennis Lancet III | 35seat Duple |

Gibson, Thomas
see Lily Coaches

Gidea Park Coaches Ltd
incl. Victory Omnibus Company
17 London Road, Romford, Essex
Garage: At address above
Allocated to LT garage: Hornchurch.

WJ	7173	Leyland Tiger TS4	32seat Cravens
WJ	7175	Leyland Tiger TS4	32seat Cravens
KPU	851	AEC Regal	32seat King & Taylor
KPU	852	AEC Regal	32seat King & Taylor
KPU	854	AEC Regal	32seat King & Taylor

Gilbert's Luxury Coaches Ltd
23 Marlborough Avenue, Edgware, Middx
Garage: G & C Garages Ltd, Peel Road, Wealdstone, Middx
Allocated to LT garage: Alperton.

CXT	536	Dennis Lancet II	32seat Metcalfe
CYL	853	Dennis Lancet II	32seat Metcalfe
JKN	885	Dennis Lancet	31seat *Body not confirmed re-registered from EV 6784.*
TMY	717	Bedford OB	29seat Duple

Gold Star Coaches
see Tyler, R. A.

Golden Miller Coaches
F. Varney, 37A York Street, Twickenham, Middx
Garage: At address above
Allocated to LT garage: Mortlake.

PL	5879	Gilford AS6	20seat Duple
CVH	240	Bedford OB	29seat Duple
SMY	152	Bedford OB	29seat Duple

Golden Star Coaches Ltd
8 Dalston Lane, E8
Garage: Barnsbury Park Garage, Liverpool Road, Islington, N1
Allocated to LT garage: Tottenham.

| GH | 3827 | AEC Regal (ex-T 289) | 32seat Duple |

Gordon, D.
see Radio Coaches

Grange, J. & Sons (Plaistow) Ltd
see Broadway Coaches

Graves, G. F. & Son
Redhill, Surrey

Garage: At address above

Allocated to LT garages: Chelsham, Reigate, Staines.

BU	7180	Leyland Tiger TS4	32seat Strachan
JJ	8824	Leyland Tiger TS4	33seat Harrington
UF	8833	Leyland Tiger TS4	33seat Strachan
UF	8843	Leyland Tiger TS4	33seat Harrington
BRK	477	Dennis Lancet II	32seat Harrington
FPE	229	Bedford WTB	26seat Willmott
KPA	271	Bedford OWB	32seat Duple
LPB	4	Bedford OB	29seat Duple
LPE	123	Bedford OB	28seat Duple

Green, A. & Sons
211 Hoe Street or 4 Rosebank Villas, High Street Walthamstow, E17

Garage: Station Garage, Baltic Yard, Hoe Street, Walthamstow, E17

Allocated to LT garages: Clayhall, Forest Gate.

NHK	984	AEC Regal III	33seat Plaxton
NNO	111	AEC Regal III	33seat Plaxton
NTW	222	Maudslay Marathon III	33seat Whitson
NVW	11	Maudslay Marathon III	33seat Santus

Green, J. G.
see Empress Coaches

Green Luxury Coaches
Walton-on-Thames, Surrey

Garage: At address above

Allocated to LT garage: Leatherhead.

ANP	611	Maudslay ML3	32seat Mulliner
LPB	749	Maudslay Marathon III	33seat Whitson
LPB	750	Maudslay Marathon III	33seat Whitson
LPH	429	Maudslay Marathon III	33seat Whitson
LPJ	129	Maudslay Marathon III	33seat Whitson

Grey Coaches
Wiggs & Son Ltd, 179A Peckham Park Road, Peckham, SE15

Garage: At address above

Allocated to LT garages: Battersea, Camberwell.

EX	4360	Tilling Stevens	35seat Watson
KJ	2914	Tilling Stevens C6OA7	32seat Roberts
KP	3053	Tilling Stevens B10	31seat Harrington
WN	8634	Tilling Stevens	32seat *Body not confirmed*
WX	2119	Tilling Stevens B10A2	32seat Roe
WX	2142	Tilling Stevens B10A2	32seat United

CUL	65	Tilling Stevens HA39	32seat Duple
DXF	612	Tilling Stevens HA39A7	32seat Duple
DXL	610	Dennis Lancet II	32seat Burlingham
HXB	200	AEC Regal	32seat Duple
HYE	800	AEC Regal	32seat Duple
JXP	100	Tilling Stevens K6LA7	33seat Dutfield

Grey Green Coaches
George Ewer & Co. Ltd, 55 Stamford Hill, Stoke Newington, N16

Garages: 55 Stamford Hill, N16
345 Mile End Road, Stepney, E1
2A Forest Road, Dalston, E8

Allocated to LT garages: Athol Street, Clayhall, Dalston, Forest Gate, Hackney, Muswell Hill, Tottenham, Upton Park.

GW	644	Leyland Tiger TS4	31seat Harrington
GW	646	Leyland Tiger TS4	31seat Harrington
UW	8901	Leyland Tiger TS2	33seat Duple
UW	8905	Leyland Tiger TS2	33seat Duple
BLY	106	Leyland Tiger TS6	32seat Harrington
BLY	667	Leyland Tiger TS6	32seat Duple
BUC	580	Leyland Tiger TS6	32seat Harrington
CUW	802	Leyland Tiger TS7	32seat Harrington
CXT	416	Leyland Tiger TS7	32seat Harrington
DXV	375	Leyland Tiger TS7	33seat Harrington
DXV	376	Leyland Tiger TS7	33seat Harrington
DXV	377	Leyland Tiger TS7	33seat Harrington
DXV	378	Leyland Tiger TS7	33seat Harrington
DXV	379	Leyland Tiger TS7	33seat Harrington
EXO	345	Leyland Tiger TS8	33seat Harrington
EXO	346	Leyland Tiger TS8	32seat Harrington
EXO	348	Leyland Tiger TS8	32seat Harrington
FLH	684	Leyland Tiger TS8	33seat Harrington
FLH	685	Leyland Tiger TS8	33seat Harrington
HLW	981	AEC Regal I	33seat Duple
HLW	982	AEC Regal I	33seat Duple
HLW	983	AEC Regal I	33seat Duple
HLW	984	AEC Regal I	33seat Duple
HLW	985	AEC Regal I	33seat Duple
HLW	986	AEC Regal I	33seat Duple
HLW	987	AEC Regal I	33seat Duple
HUU	428	Bedford OB	27seat Duple
HUU	429	Bedford OB	27seat Duple
HUU	432	Bedford OB	27seat Duple
HUU	433	Bedford OB	27seat Duple
HYE	972	Leyland PS1/1	33seat Harrington
HYH	575	Leyland PS1/1	33seat Harrington
HYH	576	Leyland PS1/1	33seat Harrington
HYH	577	Leyland PS1/1	33seat Harrington
HYO	690	Bedford OB	29seat Duple
HYP	560	Bedford OB	29seat Duple
HYP	901	Bedford OB	29seat Duple
JLH	237	Leyland PS1/1	35seat Duple
JLH	238	Leyland PS1/1	35seat Duple
JLH	239	Leyland PS1/1	35seat Duple
JLH	240	Leyland PS1/1	35seat Duple
JLH	241	Leyland PS1/1	35seat Duple

Grosvenor Coaches Ltd
F. E. Hughes, 274 Baker Street, Enfield, Middx

Garage: At address above

Allocated to LT garage: Enfield.

WH 3787	Leyland Tiger TS4	32seat Spicer
LMT 880	Bedford OWB	32seat Duple

Grove Coaches
H. R. B. Shugg, 83 Christchurch Road, Tulse Hill, SW2

Garage: Lane's Garage, 236 Norwood Road, Tulse Hill, SW2

Allocated to LT garage: Norwood.

MV 2592	Daimler CF6	32seat *Body not confirmed*
RV 1492	Tilling Stevens B10A2	32seat Park Royal
HYP 775	Bedford OB	29seat Duple
JXT 788	Austin CXB	29seat Plaxton

Grundon, C. C.
see Castle Coaches

Grundon, W. E.
1 Avery Hill Road, Eltham, SE9

Garage: At address above

Allocated to LT garage: Sidcup.

GF 1737	AEC Regal	32seat Harrington
JD 1167	AEC Regal	32seat Strachan
UW 8773	AEC Regal	33seat Beadle
HXA 290	AEC Regal I	32seat Beadle
HXA 291	AEC Regal I	32seat Beadle
MPA 689	Maudslay Marathon III	33seat Dutfield
MPA 690	Maudslay Marathon III	33seat Dutfield

Hall Brothers
13, Hercies Road, Hillingdon, Middx

Garage: 151 The Greenway, Ickenham, Middx

Allocated to LT garage: Uxbridge.

GP 3380	Leyland Tiger TS1	32seat Harrington *
GZ 728	Leyland Cheetah LZ	33seat *Body not confirmed*
JW 2744	Maudslay ML3	32seat *Body not confirmed*
JW 4901	Maudslay ML3	32seat Burlingham
MMY 696	Bedford OB	29seat Duple

* *Formerly ran for Monico Motorways (q.v.)*

Hall's Coaches
W. D. Hall Ltd, 438 Durnsford Road, Wimbledon, SW19

Garage: Bodmin Street, Wandsworth, SW18

Allocated to LT garage: Chelverton Road.

HYN 461	Bedford OB	29seat Duple
LMY 893	Bedford OB	29seat Duple
MPB 333	Bedford OB	29seat Duple
SMY 864	Bedford OB	29seat Duple

Halpin, T. W.
Rippleway Coaches/Thatched House Coaches
32 Robert Owen Road, Barking, Essex

Garage: Thatched House Garage, Ripple Road, Barking, Essex

Allocated to LT garage: Barking.

DF 8901	Guy	32seat E.C.O.C.
DF 8904	Guy	32seat E.C.O.C.
AUX 776	Bedford WTB	26seat Duple
ETW 89	Ford FC	26seat Mulliner *(utility)* *
FLE 504	Bedford WTB	26seat Duple †

* *Later recorded with Barking Coaches (q.v.)*
† *Formerly ran with Lacey's (East Ham) Ltd (q.v.)*

Hampton Coaches
A. E. Bowler
'Roebuck', Hampton Road, Hampton Hill, Middx

Garage: Alpha Garage, Alpha Road, Hampton Hill, Middx

Allocated to LT garage: Kingston.

MG 7867	Commer Commando Q4	33seat Thurgood
KLM 150	Austin CXB	29seat Mann Egerton

Hanworth Coaches
see Acorn Motors Ltd

Harold Wood Coach Services
F. W. Leach
12 Woodland Road, Harold Wood, Essex

Garage: 35 Aldborough Road, Dagenham, Essex

Allocated to LT garage: Hornchurch.

BUX 771	Bedford OWB	28seat Mulliner
CYY 308	Dennis Lancet II	35seat Duple
DMX 3	Dennis Lancet II	33seat Duple

Harrison and Hole
H. G. Harrison
112 Peckham Park Road, Peckham, SE15

Garage: S & S Motor Garage, Harders Road, Peckham, SE15

Allocated to LT garages: Nunhead, Old Kent Road.

MS 9020	Leyland Tiger TS1	33seat Alexander
BXH 678	Dennis Lancet I	32seat *Body not confirmed*
GTF 394	Maudslay Marathon II	33seat Longwell Green
KGT 17	Maudslay Marathon III	32seat Duple

Hearn, P.
238A Grays Inn Road, WC1

Garage: Northdown Street, Kings Cross, N1

Allocated to LT garages: Chalk Farm, Tottenham.

TS 8420	Leyland Lion	? seat *Body not confirmed*
WS 8009	Leyland Cheetah	32seat Duple
WS 8011	Leyland Cheetah	32seat Alexander
WV 9633	Bedford WTL	25seat *Body not confirmed*

Henry Saloon Coaches Ltd
H. Porter, 1 Broad Lane, South Tottenham, N15

Garage: Markfield Road, Tottenham Hale, N15

Allocated to LT garages: Palmers Green, Tottenham, West Green.

FG	6110	Daimler CF6	32seat Duple
FM	4504	Daimler CF6	32seat Duple
TH	3580	Leyland Tiger TS6	33seat Duple
UF	8840	Leyland Tiger TS4	32seat Harrington
UN	187	Daimler CF6	32seat Duple
HMX	175	Leyland Tiger TS8	32seat Duple
LME	665	Leyland Tiger TS7	33seat Duple
MME	153	Leyland Tiger TS4	32seat Harrington
MME	154	Leyland Tiger TS8	32seat Harrington
OML	605	Leyland PS1/1	35seat Duple
SMF	946	Leyland PS1/1	35seat Duple

Hill, F. C.
see London Road Coaches

Holder, A. R. & Sons Ltd
Railway Arches, Rolt Street, Deptford, SE8

Garages: At address above

Allocated to LT garage: Old Kent Road.

| JLG | 991 | Bedford OB | 29seat Plaxton |

Holmes, H. W.
see Horseshoe Coaches

Horseshoe Coaches
H. W. Holmes, 3 Culross Road, West Green, N15

Garages: At address above

Allocated to LT garage: Muswell Hill.

EV	6264	Leyland Tiger TS4	32seat Petty
WG	1274	Gilford 168OT	32seat Wycombe
LMG	629	Bedford OB	32seat Duple
OMY	449	Dennis Lancet	35seat Duple
SMF	380	Bedford OB	29seat Thurgood

Hounslow Star
see Garner's Coaches Ltd

Hughes, F. E.
see Grosvenor Coaches Ltd

Hunt and West
see Safeway Coaches

Hutchinson, T. J.
see Woodside Coaches

Hymar, G. A. & Weiland, A. W.
see Pathfinder Luxury Coaches

Ideal Safety Coaches
B. Ellis
106 Ripple Road, Barking

Garage:	Suffolk Road, Barking (26/1/48)	
	Sparshot Road, Barking	

Allocated to LT garages: Barking.

WG	1283	Gilford 168OT	29seat Wycombe
AGF	928	AEC Regal	32seat Strachan

Ivanhoe Coaches
Ivanhoe Hotel, 144 Copplestone Road, Camberwell, SE15

Garage:	7 Kilmarsh Road, Hammersmith, W6

Allocated to LT garages: Hammersmith, Putney Bridge.

AG	4152	Leyland Tiger TS1	32seat Wadham

J. M. Motors
J. R. Manuel
22 Warlters Road, Holloway, N7

Garage:	Metropolitan Cattle Market, Market Road, Holloway, N7

Allocated to LT garages: Holloway, West Green.

CK	3961	Leyland Tiger TS1	32seat Alexander
CK	4107	Leyland Tiger TS1	32seat Leyland
EB	9897	Dennis Lancet	32seat Willowbrook
KJ	7440	Leyland Tiger TS2	31seat Short
VA	8956	Leyland Tiger TS1	32seat Midland *
AYV	717	Leyland Cub (ex-C 1)	20seat LPTB†
CUC	104	Bedford WTB	26seat *Body not confirmed*
DAW	994	Commer Commando	30seat Harrington
EXA	63	Dennis Lancet II	33seat Duple §
EXF	921	Leyland Cheetah	32seat Harrington
FNN	669	Leyland Cheetah	32seat Brush
JXH	169	Commer Commando	30seat Allweather
JXN	626	Commer Commando	30seat Allweather
KGW	566	Commer Commando	30seat Allweather

* Later sold to Wayfarer Coaches (q.v.)
† Later sold to Overland Lismore Coaches Ltd (q.v.)
§ Formerly ran for Wright Bros (London) Ltd (q.v.)

Jacobs, I.
see Criterion Coaches Ltd

Jays Coaches
4 Church Road, Harold Park, Essex

Garage:	Maylands Garage, Colchester Road, Harold Park, Essex

Allocated to LT garage: Hornchurch.

DF	8902	Guy	30seat Beadle

Jewell's Coaches
21 Lindfield Road, Croydon, Surrey

Garage: George Street, Croydon, Surrey

Allocated to LT garage: Croydon.

FOY	323	Bedford OB	29seat Duple

Jones, A.
see Popular Coaches Ltd

Julius and Lockwood
Porson Street Garage, Lewisham, SE13

Garage: At address above

Allocated to LT garage: Catford.

JD	1378	AEC Regal	32seat Strachan
VS	2094	AEC Regal	32seat Harrington
AGJ	614	AEC Regal	32seat Short
DXD	784	Bedford WTB	25seat Duple

Kilsby, N. J. & K. B.
3 Dunholme Road, Lower Edmonton, N9

Garage: Angel Garage, Angel Road, Edmonton, N18

Allocated to LT garage: Enfield.

CRR	820	Leyland Cub	23seat Brush

King, W. & Sons Ltd
see Emerald Coaches Ltd

Knight, R. F.
see White Line Coaches.

Knowler's Coaches Ltd
Knowler Brothers
3 Culross Road, West Green, N15

Garage: Haslemere Garage, Highbridge Street, Waltham Cross

Allocated to LT garage: Enfield.

AYH	297	Leyland Lion LT5A	35seat Birch

Lacey's (East Ham) Ltd
222 Barking Road, East Ham, E6

Garage: 42 Ranelagh Road, East Ham, E6

Allocated to LT garage: Barking.

BHV	792	Bedford OB	29seat Duple
BHV	793	Bedford OB	29seat Duple
FLE	504	Bedford WTB	26seat Duple *
JTE	704	Leyland PS1/1	33seat Burlingham
SML	467	Bedford OB	29seat Duple †
TMK	640	Bedford OB	29seat Duple

* *Later ran for T. W. Halpin (q.v.)*

† *Later ran for Barking Coaches Ltd (q.v.)*

Lambird, G.
see Carshalton & Wallington Coaches Ltd

Lansdowne Luxury Coaches Ltd
502 High Road, Leytonstone, E11

Garage: 130/134 Union Road, Leytonstone, E11

Allocated to LT garage: Forest Gate.

BU	6465	Leyland Tiger TS2	32seat *Body not confirmed*
GX	166	AEC Regal	32seat Duple
IIG	1024	AEC Hegent	50seat Roe *
HG	1223	AEC Regent	50seat Brush *
JX	5264	AEC Regent	56seat Park Royal *
JX	6427	AEC Regent	56seat Park Royal *
EPU	120	Tilling Stevens	32seat Duple

* Double deck

Latham, A. W.
see Enterprise Coaches

Lawrence Bros (Transport) Ltd
Pickard Street, City Road, EC1

Garage: At address above

Allocated to LT garage: Holloway.

HUV	768	Leyland Tiger TS4	32seat Harrington
JXD	750	Bedford OB	28seat Mulliner
KGT	598	Commer Commando	30seat Pearson

Leach, F. W.
see Harold Wood Coach Services

Lee's Luxury Coaches Ltd
R. M. Lee, 36 High Street, Barnet, Herts

Garage: 16 High Street, Barnet, Herts

Allocated to LT garage: Potters Bar.

BRO	420	AEC Regal	32seat Duple
DRO	179	AEC Regal	32seat Duple
HUR	621	Dennis Lancet III	35seat Duple

Leighton Coach Co. Ltd
2 High Road, Ilford, Essex

Garage: 27A Oaklands Park Avenue, Ilford, Essex

Allocated to LT garages: Barking, Hornchurch, Seven Kings.

AND	846	Leyland Tiger TS4	33seat Duple
JTW	333	Bedford OWB	32seat Duple *(utility)*
JTW	334	Bedford OWB	26seat Duple *(utility)*
JTW	335	Bedford OWB	28seat Duple *(utility)*
LTW	461	Bedford OB	29seat Duple

Lewis, C. G.
Lewis's Safety Coaches, 109 Pelton Road, Greenwich, SE10

Garage: Hoskin Street, Greenwich, SE10

Allocated to LT garages: Athol Street, Clayhall, Hackney, Old Kent Road.

MV	2668	Leyland Tiger TS4	32seat Duple
VD	4449	Leyland Tiger TS7	39seat Leyland
DLX	912	Leyland Tiger TS7	32seat Duple
DLX	913	Leyland Tiger TS7	33seat Duple
EXH	14	Leyland Tiger TS8	33seat Duple
EXT	615	Leyland Tiger TS8	33seat Duple
HXX	47	Maudslay Marathon II	33seat Duple
HXX	48	Maudslay Marathon II	33seat Duple
HXX	49	Maudslay Marathon II	33seat Duple
HXX	50	Maudslay Marathon II	33seat Duple
JXH	515	Leyland PS1/1	33seat Duple
SML	597	Leyland PS1/1	33seat Duple

Lily Coaches
Thomas Gibson, 124 Church Street, Lower Edmonton, N9

Garage: Weir Hall Garage, Cambridge Circus, Edmonton, N18

Allocated to LT garages: Enfield, Palmers Green, Tottenham.

JMC	987	AEC Regal I	32seat Duple
MMY	104	AEC Regal I	33seat Duple
MMY	105	AEC Regal I	33seat Duple
OMY	405	AEC Regal I	35seat Duple
SME	229	AEC Regal I	35seat Duple
SME	230	AEC Regal I	35seat Duple
SML	10	AEC Regal III	33seat Duple
SMY	262	Bedford OB	29seat Duple

London Road Coaches
F. C. Hill, 10 Mackenzie Street, Slough, Bucks

Garages: Bridge Garage, 122 Green Lanes, Palmers Green, N13
                     499 Hackney Road, Bethnal Green, E2

Allocated to LT garages: Hackney, West Green.

WH	1299	Leyland Tiger TS1	32seat Harrington
AXK	845	AEC Regal	32seat Harrington
BXN	426	AEC Regal	32seat Harrington
CBE	616	Bedford OWB	32seat Duple *(utility)*
EHO	919	Bedford OWB	32seat Duple

Longman, Edwin Ltd
see Elms Longman Motor Services Ltd

Lucky Line Coaches Ltd
11 Whitchurch Avenue, Edgware, Middx,

Garage: Stonegrove Garage, Edgware, Middx

Allocated to LT garages: Cricklewood, Harrow Weald.

UK	8450	AEC Regal	31seat Burlingham
EJB	645	Commer Commando	30seat Allweather
OML	97	Commer Commando	30seat Harrington
SMY	22	Commer Commando	30seat Harrington
SMY	294	Bedford OB	29seat Duple

Majestic Luxury Coaches Ltd
A. A. Tozer
55A Leytonstone Road, Stratford, E15

Garage: Baltic Garage, 211 Hoe Street, Walthamstow, E17

Allocated to LT garages: Forest Gate, Hackney, Leyton, Tottenham.

VN 7172	Albion PV	31seat *Body not confirmed* *
HYU 82	Maudslay Marathon III	33seat Whitson
JXB 23	Maudslay Marathon III	33seat Whitson
JXD 214	Maudslay Marathon III	33seat Whitson
LPB 748	Bedford OB	27seat Whitson *
LPF 249	Bedford OB	27seat Whitson *
MEV 799	Maudslay Marathon II	33seat Westnor

* On loan from Green Luxury, Walton

Manny, L. Ltd
18 Goodwood Mansions, Stockwell Park Walk, Lambeth, SW9

Garage: Maskell's Garage, 297 Brixton Road, Brixton, SW9

Allocated to LT garage: Streatham.

JXL 558	Bedford OB	29seat Duple

Manuel, J. R.
see J. M. Motors

Margo's
R. Margo (see also Bexleyheath Transport)

Garage: not listed in LT schedules (cf. Bexleyheath Transport)

Allocated to LT garage: Catford.

FV 448	Daimler CF6	33seat Duple (fitted with AEC Reliance radiator)
TMK 74	AEC Regal I	35seat Strachan

Martindale Coaches
see Roberts & Dickenson

McCafferty, P. F.
see Avonley Coaches

McCormack, R.
7 Monmouth Road, Dagenham, Essex

Garage: Bull Garage, Rainham Road, Dagenham, Essex

Allocated to LT garage: Hornchurch.

CK 4292	Leyland Tiger TS2	32seat Leyland
CK 4739	Leyland Tiger TS6	32seat English Electric
FV 5591	Leyland Tiger TS6	32seat Burlingham
RN 8859	Leyland Tiger	33seat Duple
HRF 30	Leyland Tiger TS8	35seat Willowbrook

Merry's Luxury Coaches
Merry & Wilson Coach Co.
18 Kingsley Road, Upton Lane, E7 and 426 Central Park Road, East Ham, E6

Garage: 18 Kingsley Road, Upton Lane, E7

Allocated to LT garages: Athol Street, Forest Gate.

CS	1998	Albion Valkyrie	31seat Scottish Aviation

Messenger, G. D.
see Robin & Rambler Coaches Ltd

Modern Super Coaches
87C Hertford Road, Lower Edmonton, N9

Garage: 31 Lancaster Road, Enfield, Middx

Allocated to LT garages: Enfield, Palmers Green.

CML	839	Bedford WTL	25seat Thurgood
KMG	450	Bedford WTB	26seat Thurgood
SMF	961	Bedford OB	29seat Duple
SML	276	Bedford OB	29seat Thurgood

Monico Motorways
6 Willes Road, Kentish Town, NW5

Garage: Flight's Garage, Parkhurst Road, Holloway, N7

Allocated to LT garage: West Green.

GP	3380	Leyland Tiger TS1	32seat Harrington *
JG	6524	Leyland Tiger TS7	32seat Park Royal
DNT	90	Bedford OB	28seat Mulliner
EWT	806	Leyland Tiger TS7	31seat English Electric
GAA	872	Bedford OB	29seat Wadham
JXC	780	Dennis Lancet III	33seat Duple

* Later ran for Hall Brothers (q.v.)

Mountain Transport Services Ltd
Manresa Road, Chelsea, SW3

Garage: At address above

Allocated to LT garages: Hammersmith, Mortlake, Putney Bridge.

KJ	1612	TSM C60A7	31seat Beadle
RC	408	SOS IM4	32seat Brush
RC	409	SOS IM4	32seat Brush
RC	410	SOS IM4	32seat Brush
RC	426	SOS IM4	32seat Brush
CJD	596	Bedford OYD	29seat Bonallack
JXK	884	Commer	32seat *Body not confirmed*
KGT	977	Crossley SD42/7	33seat Santus
KGW	20	Austin CXB	31seat Mann Egerton

Nealon, R. E.
see Cosy Coaches

New Karrymore Coaches Ltd
see Ansell's Coaches

Omnia Transporters Ltd
22 William IV Street, WC2

Garage: 72 Perry Vale, Forest Hill, SE23

Allocated to LT garages: Bromley, Catford.

DX 8047	Tilling Stevens B10A2	35seat *Body not confirmed*
DX 8049	Tilling Stevens B10A2	35seat *Body not confirmed*
DX 8092	Tilling Stevens B10A2	35seat *Body not confirmed*
DX 8590	Tilling Stevens B10A2	32seat *Body not confirmed*
ER 8886	Leyland Lion PLSC3	34seat E.C.O.C. *(rebodied)*
VE 306	Leyland Lion PLSC3	33seat E.C.O.C. *(rebodied)*
YF 1906	Tilling Stevens B9A	36seat *Body not confirmed*

Orange Coaches (Keith & Boyle) Ltd
Orange Luxury Coaches
30 Harleyford Road, Lambeth, SE11

Garage: Terminal House, 80 Clapham Road, SW9

Allocated to LT garages: Battersea, Hammersmith, Middle Row, Victoria.

HLX 836	Bedford OB	29seat Duple
HXB 711	Bedford OB	27seat Duple
HXB 713	Bedford OB	27seat Duple
HXB 714	Bedford OB	27seat Duple
HXB 715	Bedford OB	27seat Duple
HXB 717	Bedford OB	27seat Duple
HXB 721	Bedford OB	27seat Duple
HXB 723	Bedford OB	27seat Duple
HXB 726	Bedford OB	27seat Duple
HXB 727	Bedford OB	27seat Duple
HYH 556	Bedford OB	27seat Duple
HYH 557	Bedford OB	27seat Duple
HYH 560	Bedford OB	27seat Duple
HYH 570	Bedford OB	27seat Duple
HYH 919	Bedford OB	27seat Duple

Overland Lismore Coaches Ltd
22 Oak Village, Kentish Town, NW5 (or 69 Roderick Road, Kentish Town, NW5)

Garage: Haverstock Road Garage, Malden Road, Kentish Town, NW5

Allocated to LT garages: Chalk Farm, Holloway.

DB 9384	Tilling Stevens B10AZ	31seat E.C.O.C.
KX 8644	AEC Regal (ex-T 366)	33seat Duple *(rebodied May 1939)* *
AYV 717	Leyland Cub (ex-C 1)	20seat LPTB †

* *Formerly ran with Clarke's Luxury Coaches (q.v.)*
† *Formerly ran with J. M. Motors (q.v.)*

Paddington Transport Services Ltd
9 Great Western Road, Paddington, W9

Garage: 13 Shirland Mews, Fernhead Road, Paddington, W9

Allocated to LT garage: Middle Row.

CS 117	Gilford Hera 176SD	32seat Wycombe
CS 3372	Leyland Cheetah LZ2	32seat Alexander
UR 6802	AEC Regal	32seat Harrington

Parker's Coaches (Kingsbury)
9 Meadowbank Road, Church Lane, Kingsbury, NW9

Garage: Boakes Yard, Roe Green, Kingsbury, NW9

Allocated to LT garage: Hendon.

RV	1495	Tilling Stevens B10AZ	32seat Park Royal

Parkside Coaches
F. E. Taylor and W. H. Edwards, 125 Dawlish Drive, Ilford, Essex

Garage: At address above

Allocated to LT garage: Barking.

KJ	6981	Thornycroft Cygnet	32seat Strachan
BAB	799	Maudslay ML5B	33seat Grose

Pathfinder Luxury Coaches
G. A. Hymar and A. W. Weiland
Grove Farm, High Road, Chadwell Heath, Essex

Garage: At address above

Allocated to LT garages: Barking, Hornchurch, Seven Kings.

LVX	467	Maudslay Marathon II	33seat Whitson
LVX	468	Maudslay Marathon III	33seat Whitson
MEV	391	Maudslay Marathon II	33seat Whitson
MNO	144	Maudslay Marathon III	33seat Whitson

Pearl and Gunn
The Fairway, 8 The Fairway, Mill Hill, NW7

Garage: Fallowfield & Britten, 393 Bethnal Green Road, Bethnal Green, E2

Allocated to LT garage: Dalston.

AGP	494	Albion Valiant	32seat Duple

Popular Coaches Ltd
A. Jones, 216 St Leonards Road, Poplar, E14

Garage: At address above

Allocated to LT garage: Clayhall.

CXT	690	Dennis Lancet II	33seat Duple
DYO	375	Dennis Lancet II	33seat Duple
HXY	214	Bedford OB	29seat Duple
HXY	215	Bedford OB	29seat Duple

Porter, H.
see Henry Saloon Coaches Ltd

Premier Omnibus Company
103–105 Queens Avenue, Watford, Herts

Garage: At address above

Allocated to LT garage: St Albans.

GF	547	AEC Regal (ex-T 119)	35seat Thurgood *(rebodied May 1939)*
GF	581	AEC Regal (ex-T 64)	35seat Thurgood *(rebodied May 1939)*
UR	6895	AEC Regal	35seat Thurgood
VU	425	AEC Regal	32seat *Body not confirmed*
JAR	954	Bedford OB	29seat Thurgood

Pritchard, John
Norway Wharf, Commercial Road, Poplar, E14

Garage: At address above

Allocated to LT garage: Dalston.

HYO	97	Bedford OB	29seat Duple
TMV	503	Bedford OB	29seat Duple

Progress Coaches
A. E. Fox, 304A Latimer Road, North Kensington, W10

Garage: 296 Latimer Road, North Kensington, W10

Allocated to LT garages: Shepherds Bush, Willesden.

HYM	329	Maudslay Marathon III	33seat Whitson

Progress Coaches
Freemantle & Dobson, 16 Clyde Avenue, Sanderstead

Garage: Hamsey Green garage, Limpsfield Road, Sanderstead

Allocated to LT garage: Croydon.

XJ	1085	Tilling Stevens B39A4	32seat Duple *
BHJ	676	AEC Regal	32seat Harrington
DLT	11	Bedford WTB	25seat Duple

* Body is recorded as Duple (utility) but photograph suggests otherwise

R.A.C.S.
Royal Arsenal Co-operative Society, 147 Powis Street, Woolwich, SE18

Garages: The Driftway, Streatham Road, Mitcham, Surrey
                         Church Street, Woolwich, SE18

Allocated to LT garages: Catford, Forest Gate, Plumstead, Streatham.

DYO	298	Leyland Tiger	32seat Beadle
HXX	534	AEC Regal III	32seat Beadle
HXX	535	AEC Regal III	32seat Beadle
HXX	536	AEC Regal III	32seat Beadle
HXX	537	AEC Regal III	32seat Beadle
HXX	538	AEC Regal III	32seat Beadle
HXX	539	AEC Regal III	32seat Beadle
HXX	540	AEC Regal III	32seat Duple
HXX	541	AEC Regal III	32seat Duple
JXP	488	Dennis Lancet III	35seat Whitson

Radio Coaches
D. Gordon, 53/57 Bishopscote Road, Luton, Beds.

Garages: 78A Grosvenor Park Road, Walthamstow, E17
                         17 Sidmouth Mews, Harrison Street, Grays Inn Road, WC1

Allocated to LT garages: Chalk Farm, Clayhall, Forest Gate, Holloway, Tottenham.

FA	5849	Guy Arab	34seat Brush
FA	5855	Guy Arab	34seat Brush
KP	8372	Leyland Lion LT1	32seat Ransomes
TG	1152	AEC Regal	35seat Metcalfe
ACJ	434	Bedford WTB	26seat Duple
AUX	891	Bedford WTB	28seat Duple
DKB	809	Leyland Cheetah	32seat *Body not confirmed*
DNO	724	Ford	27seat *Body not confirmed*

DOX	601	Leyland Lion LT8	35seat Burlingtham
EJU	832	Maudslay Marathon III	33seat Whitson
EKV	416	Commer Q4	30seat Plaxton
ENM	682	Albion PH115	26seat *Body not confirmed*
FMJ	44	Daimler CVD6	33seat Yorkshire Yachtbuilders
GBM	719	Daimler CVD6	33seat Plaxton
JAL	82	Commer Q4	30seat Plaxton

Ranelagh Coaches
C. F. Seyfred
130 Market Street, East Ham, E6

Garage: Nelson Street, East Ham, E6

Allocated to LT garage: Upton Park.

GN	9745	AEC Regal	32seat Hoyle
HV	1967	AEC Regal	32seat Barking Garage & Engineering Co. Ltd
WG	2314	Gilford Hera L176S	32seat Wycombe
CBA	766	AEC Regal	33seat Plaxton
EXT	618	Leyland Tiger TS1	32seat Duple

Ray (Edgware) Ltd
Ray's Coaches
27 Garden City, Edgware, Middx

Garage: 288 Hale Lane, Edgware, Middx

Allocated to LT garage: Edgware.

MMT	879	Bedford OB	29seat Duple
MMT	880	Bedford OB	27seat Duple
SML	696	Bedford OB	29seat Duple

Rayner's Coachways Ltd
7 High Street, Feltham, Middx

Garages: 596 London Road, Ashford, Middx
                  Baber Bridge Garage, Hounslow Road, Feltham, Middx

Allocated to LT garage: Hounslow.

AV	6486	Albion Valkyrie PW67	32seat Walker (Aberdeen)
GU	3695	AEC Reliance	33seat Duple
GZ	729	Leyland Cheetah	31seat Duple
VP	9531	Maudslay ML6A	32seat Buckingham
AYH	350	Maudslay ML3	32seat Duple

Red Line Continental Motorways Ltd
335 Portobello Road, North Kensington, W10

Garage: At address above

Allocated to LT garages: Middle Row, Twickenham, Victoria, Willesden.

FS	6008	Daimler CP6	32seat Burlingham
CXM	711	Leyland Tiger TS7	21seat Strachan
HYN	566	Commer Commando	20seat Strachan
HYU	539	Leyland PS1/1	25seat Strachan
JGY	448	AEC Regal III	32seat Strachan

Rippleway Coaches
see Halpin, T. W.

Roberts & Dickenson
Ashford Belle/Martindale Coaches
4 Fairfield Rd, Kingston, Surrey/38 Fairholme Rd. Ashford, Middx
Garage: Bentall's Garage, Wood Street, Kingston, Surrey
Allocated to LT garages: Kingston, Twickenham.

KJ	1863	Commer Invader	20seat Chatham Motor Co.
KR	1744	Leyland Tiger TS2	32seat Short
MS	9061	Leyland Lion LT1	32seat Alexander
PJ	3827	AEC Regal	35seat Burlingham *(utility)*
TX	9498	AEC Regal	35seat Burlingham *(utility)*
UF	8834	Leyland Tiger TS4	31seat Harrington
VH	6530	AEC Regal	32seat Brush
AKL	667	Commer Centaur	20seat Harrington
CNO	75	Gilford Hera 176S	29seat Wycombe
CNO	76	Gilford Hera 176S	29seat Wycombe

Robin & Rambler Coaches Ltd
G. D. Messenger
12 St John's Hill, Clapham Junction, SW11
Garage: 324 Battersea Park Road, Battersea, SW11
Allocated to LT garages: Camberwell, Hammersmith.

HYE	762	Bedford OB	29seat Whitson
HYO	356	Maudslay Marathon III	33seat Whitson
HYO	357	Maudslay Marathon III	33seat Whitson
JXB	321	Bedford OB	29seat Whitson
JXB	322	Bedford OB	29seat Whitson
JXE	956	Bedford OB	29seat Whitson

Rose Transport Co. Ltd
44 Hornsey Road, Holloway, N7
Garage: 45 Hornsey Road, Holloway, N7
Allocated to LT garage: Holloway.

EUM	900	Dennis Lancet II	32seat Dennis
HXX	972	Bedford OB	29seat Duple
JXT	615	Bedford OB	29seat Woodall Nicholson

Roseland
see Davis, Fred & Sons

Safeway Coaches
Hunt and West
142 Maynards Road, Walthamstow, E17
Garage: 146 Grove Road, Walthamstow, E17
Allocated to LT garages: Athol Street, Dalston, Forest Gate, Tottenham.

DM	9308	Thornycroft Cygnet	32seat Thurgood
OW	3434	Thornycroft Daring	56seat Park Royal *
AHR	647	Leyland Cub	20seat Weymann
DXV	882	Albion Victor	29seat Strachan
NPU	424	Bedford OB	29seat Duple

* *Double deck*

Sargent, H. J.
Mrs Janet Sargent
32 Cantelupe Road, East Grinstead, West Sussex

Garage: Central Garage (Croydon) Ltd, Rear of Town Hall, Croydon.

Allocated to LT garages: Croydon, Sutton.

CNJ	347	Bedford OWB	27seat Duple *(utility)*
CNJ	887	Bedford OWB	27seat Duple *(utility)*
CPM	121	Bedford OWB	27seat Duple *(utility)*

Sceptre Coaches
Bingley Bros Ltd
3 Dunsany Road, Hammersmith, W14

Garage: Downs Place, Hammersmith, W6

Allocated to LT garages: Hammersmith, Putney Bridge.

HYE	927	Bedford OB	29seat Duple
HYN	700	Bedford OB	29seat Duple

Seyfred, C. F.
see Ranelagh Coaches

Shirley Coaches
A. Bennett & Sons
1 Sandpits Road, Shirley, Surrey

Garage: Peall Road, Croydon, Surrey

Allocated to LT garage: Croydon

GH	623	AEC Regal (ex-T 139)	32seat Burlingham *(rebodied)*

Shugg, H. R. B.
see Grove Coaches

Smith, F. W. B
see Argosy Super Coaches

Smith's Luxury Coaches
A. E. Smith (South East Area)
20 Mill Road, Reading, Berks

Garage: Pickford's Garage, Coronation Road, Park Royal, NW10

Allocated to LT garages: Alperton, Hammersmith, Hanwell, Shepherds Bush, Willesden.

CS	3352	Leyland Cheetah	33seat Alexander
CS	3370	Leyland Cheetah	33seat Alexander
WS	8001	Leyland Cheetah	33seat Alexander
WS	8007	Leyland Cheetah	33seat Alexander
WS	8014	Leyland Cheetah	33seat Alexander
WS	8018	Leyland Cheetah	33seat Alexander
WS	8019	Leyland Cheetah	33seat Alexander
WS	8022	Leyland Cheetah	33seat Alexander
WS	8025	Leyland Cheetah	33seat Alexander
WS	8027	Leyland Cheetah	33seat Alexander
WS	8029	Leyland Cheetah	33seat Alexander
WS	8036	Leyland Cheetah	33seat Alexander
WS	8045	Leyland Cheetah	33seat Alexander
CRD	585	Leyland Tiger TS7	33seat Burlingham

Stanley, Ben Ltd
Burwood Road, Hersham, Surrey

Garage:	At address above

Allocated to LT garage: Kingston.

JPL	163	Bedford OWB	32seat Duple
KPA	298	Bedford OWB	32seat Duple *(utility)*
KPB	265	Bedford OWB	27seat Duple *(utility)*

Star Luxury Coaches
Burfoot and Jones, 36 Swan Road, Feltham (formerly Hanworth), Middx

Garage:	27 Swan Road, Feltham (formerly Hanworth), Middx

Allocated to LT garage: Hounslow.

KR	9207	Morris Viceroy	25seat Harrington
CCG	229	Ford V8	20seat *Body not confirmed*
FRY	962	Commer Q4	30seat Pearson

Streatham Vale Luxury Coaches
1 Marian Road, Streatham, SW16

Garage:	At address above

Allocated to LT garage: Streatham.

BXH	126	Thornycroft Cygnet	32seat Thurgood
CPH	230	Thornycroft Cygnet	32seat Thurgood
ELP	98	Bedford WTB	26seat Duple
EUW	54	Bedford WTB	25seat Duple

Sunbeam
C. J. Worsley, 277 Wood Street, Walthamstow, E17

Garage:	At address above

Allocated to LT garages: Forest Gate, Leyton.

GH	3817	AEC Regal (ex-T 194)	33seat Short
GN	4417	AEC Regal	33seat E.C.O.C.
AAL	159	Leyland Cub	26seat *Body not confirmed*
AWJ	232	AEC Ranger	29seat Cravens
AWJ	234	AEC Ranger	29seat Cravens

Superior Coaches Ltd
548A High Road, Tottenham, N17

Garage:	Fox Garage, Forster Road, Tottenham, N17

Allocated to LT garage: Enfield.

AG	6505	AEC Regal	32seat Mains
WN	4767	AEC Regent	32seat Beadle *
HMX	552	AEC Regent	32seat *Body not confirmed* *
LMY	260	AEC Regal	32seat Park Royal
MME	45	AEC Regent	32seat Burlingham *
OML	459	AEC Regal	32seat Bush & Twiddy
SML	139	AEC Regal (ex-T195)	32seat *Body not confirmed* *
TMG	687	AEC Regent	33seat Barnaby *
TMG	688	AEC Regent	33seat Barnaby *
TMG	690	AEC Regal	35seat Churchill
TMG	691	AEC Regal	35seat Churchill

* Regent with single deck body. HMX 552 later ran with S. V. Twigg (q.v.), MME 45 previously registered CPH 625, and SML 139 GF 577.

Surrell, L. D., Ltd
62A Highfield Avenue, Wembley, NW9

Garage:	At address above
Allocated to LT garage:	Cricklewood.

FS	6007	Daimler CP6	32seat Burlingham

Sydenham Coaches
W. F. Butler, 120 Sydenham Road, Sydenham, SE26

Garage:	At address above
Allocated to LT garages:	Catford.

WX	8989	Tilling Stevens B49A7	32seat E.C.O.C.
YG	1706	AEC Regal	33seat Burlingham
HYH	912	Bedford OB	27seat Duple

Tatnall Brothers Ltd
see Avondale Safety Coaches

Taylor, F. E. & Edwards, W. H.
see Parkside Coaches

Thatched House Coaches
see Halpin, T. W.

Thorne Bros
D. H. Thorne, 148/150 Brixton Hill, Brixton, SW2

Garage:	At address above
Allocated to LT garage:	Norwood.

BXH	778	Dennis Lancet 1	32seat *Body not confirmed*
CYL	216	Dennis Lancet	33seat Dennis
EXF	199	Dennis Lancet I	32seat Dennis
MML	496	Bedford OB	29seat Duple
SMF	632	Bedford OB	29seat Duple
SMY	920	Bedford OB	29seat Duple

Thorpe Coaches Ltd
46 Ewellhurst Road, Ilford, Essex

Garage:	814 High Road, Leyton, E10
Allocated to LT garages:	Dalston, Leyton, Upton Park.

DPL	448	Dennis Lancet	33seat Strachan
EXO	797	Dennis Lancet II	32seat Duple
GLU	601	Dennis Lancet	32seat Strachan
MPU	348	Bedford OB	29seat Duple

Tonge, L.
'Elmfield', Elstree, Herts

Garage:	High Street, Elstree, Herts
Allocated to LT garage:	Edgware.

No details of vehicles traced but the company was acquired by R. A. Tyler (see overleaf) in June 1948 and the vehicles may have been acquired also.

Topple's Coaches
D. W. Topple Rainham (Essex ?)

Garages:	Not recorded on LT lists.	
	(R. Lunn records as running for a very short period in 1949)	

Allocated to LT garage: Victoria

WG	333	Gilford 168OT	32seat Wycombe
BHR	138	?	26seat *Body not confirmed*
BWM	552	Albion Victor	26seat *Body not confirmed*

Tozer, A. A.
see Majestic Luxury Coaches Ltd

Try, R.
see Windsorian

Twigg, S. V.
County Coaches, County Garage, Rayleigh, Essex

Garage: 28 Penrhyn Avenue, Walthamstow, E17

Allocated to LT garage: Tottenham.

GK	3411	Gilford 168OT	32seat Wycombe
HMX	552	AEC Regent	32seat *Body not confirmed* *
NTW	86	Leyland Cub SKP	20seat *Body not confirmed*

* *Single deck body, formerly ran with Superior Coaches (q.v.)*

Tyler, R. A.
Gold Star Coaches *(see also L. Tonge)***, 8 Wilson Cottages, High Street, Elstree, Herts**

Garage: High Street, Elstree, Herts

Allocated to LT garage: Edgware.

FEH	625	Dennis Lancet II	39seat Willowbrook
JAE	332	Bedford OWB	28seat Duple *(utility)*

Ubique Coaches
144 Portnall Road, Paddington, W9

Garage: At address above

Allocated to LT garage: Shepherds Bush.

JXE	296	Maudslay Marathon III	33seat Westnor

United Service Transport Co. Ltd
including Blue Belle Motors Ltd / L. Adnams, 143 Clapham Road, SW9

Garages: At address above and High Street, Merton

Allocated to LT garages: Battersea, Chelverton Road, Hanwell, Merton, Mortlake, Norwood, Putney Bridge.

CK	4195	Leyland Tiger TS1	32seat Harrington
EA	8300	Leyland Tiger TS7	32seat Duple
EV	1780	AEC Regal	32seat Duple
GC	7407	AEC Regal	32seat Duple
GF	5126	AEC Regal	32seat Duple
GJ	8071	AEC Regal	32seat Duple
CLC	695	Leyland Tiger TS7	32seat Duple
HYF	532	Bedford OB	27seat Duple
HYK	235	Bedford OB	27seat Duple

HYO	260	Leyland PS1/1	33seat Strachan
HYO	261	Leyland PS1/1	33seat Strachan
HYO	262	Leyland PS1/1	33seat Strachan
HYP	210	Bedford OB	27seat Duple
HYP	328	Leyland PS1/1	33seat Strachan
HYP	329	Leyland PS1/1	33seat Strachan
HYP	330	Leyland PS1/1	33seat Strachan
HYR	192	Leyland PS1/1	33seat Strachan
HYR	193	Leyland PS1/1	33seat Strachan
HYR	194	Leyland PS1/1	33seat Strachan
HYR	440	Leyland PS1/1	33seat Strachan
HYR	586	Leyland PS1/1	33seat Strachan
HYR	782	Leyland PS1/1	33seat Duple
HYR	783	Leyland PS1/1	33seat Duple
KPA	139	Leyland Tiger TS7	32seat Harrington
LPC	851	Bedford OB	27seat Duple
MMH	618	Bedford OB	27seat Duple
MMH	619	Bedford OB	27seat Duple

Universal Coaches Ltd
20 The Broadway, Lower Edmonton, N9

Garage: Monmouth Road, Hertford Road, Lower Edmonton, N9

Allocated to LT garages: Palmers Green, Tottenham.

LML	154	Bedford OWB	32seat Mulliner
LML	486	Bedford OWB	32seat Duple
LMT	602	Bedford	?seat *Body not confirmed*
MTW	985	Maudslay Marathon	33seat Whitson *
MVX	881	Maudslay Marathon II	35seat Whitson *

* Acquired from Dix Luxury Coaches November 1948 (q.v.)

Usher's Saloon Coaches
Chas. T. Usher, 55 Medway Road, Bow, E3

Garage: 24 Bow Road, Bow, E3

Allocated to LT garages: Barking, Dalston.

BMG	101	Leyland Lion LT5A	32seat Beadle

Valliant Direct Motor Coaches Ltd
38 Uxbridge Road, Ealing, W5

Garage: At address above

Allocated to LT garages: Alperton, Hammersmith, Hanwell, Willesden.

AG	4145	Leyland Tiger TS1	32seat Brush
PV	4636	Leyland Lion LT8	35seat Duple
VA	8890	Leyland Tiger TS1	32seat Midland
WN	9804	Leyland Lion LT7	32seat Duple
CCD	727	Leyland Tiger TS7	32seat Harrington
CCD	750	Leyland Tiger TS7	32seat Harrington
CMH	775	Leyland Tiger TS7	32seat Duple
DXT	595	Leyland Tiger TS7	32seat Strachan (?)
EYF	866	Leyland Tiger TS8	32seat Duple
EYF	867	Leyland Tiger TS8	32seat Metcalfe
EYL	862	Leyland Tiger TS7	32seat Duple
FMP	56	AEC Regal	32seat Strachan
LMG	526	Leyland Tiger TS8	32seat Duple
LMT	82	Leyland Tiger TS4	32seat Duple

MMP	815	Bedford OB	29seat Duple
MMY	454	AEC Regal	32seat Strachan
OML	293	AEC Regal	33seat Strachan
OML	294	AEC Regal	33seat Strachan
OMT	80	Leyland Tiger TS7	32seat Burlingham
OMT	456	Leyland Tiger TS6	32seat *Body not confirmed*
OMT	555	Leyland Tiger TS7	32seat Valliant
SME	12	Maudslay Marathon III	33seat Whitson
SME	323	Leyland Lion LT7	34seat *Body not confirmed*
			(previously registered CML 981).
SMF	605	Bedford OB	29seat Duple
SML	50	Maudslay Marathon III	35seat Whitson
SML	399	Leyland PS1/1	33seat Strachan

Varney, F.
see Golden Miller Coaches

Venture Transport (Hendon) Ltd
Waterloo Road, Cricklewood, NW2

Garage: At address above

Allocated to LT garages: Cricklewood, Hanwell, Hendon, Shepherds Bush.

DMX	198	Leyland Tiger TS7	32seat Duple
OMT	373	Leyland PS1/1	33seat Duple
SME	81	AEC Regal I	32seat Brush
SME	82	AEC Regal I	32seat Brush
SME	83	AEC Regal I	32seat Brush
SME	84	AEC Regal I	32seat Brush

Victory Omnibus Company
see Gidea Park Coaches Ltd

Viney's Luxury Coaches
264 High Road, South Tottenham., N15

Garage: Rowley's Yard, Woodside Park Road, South Tottenham, N15

Allocated to LT garages: Muswell Hill, West Green.

BU	9450	Leyland Tiger TS7	35seat Duple *(rebodied 1947)*
FV	49	Leyland Tiger TS1	33seat Duple *(rebodied 1947)*
EYE	592	Leyland Tiger TS1	33seat Duple
SMF	530	Bedford OB	29seat Duple
TMG	732	Bedford OB	29seat Duple
TMG	847	Daimler CVD6	35seat Thurgood
TMY	677	Crossley SD42/7	33seat Strachan

Viola
Bermondsey. On original list but may not have operated

Garage: Not recorded on any LT lists.

Allocated to LT garages: Old Kent Road (but doubtful if ever operated).

No details of vehicles traced

Watkins, W.
Fleetwood, Staplehurst, Kent

Garages: Astoria Garage, Gracefield Gardens, Streatham, SW18
Thomas Kent, 16 Westbridge Road, Battersea, SW11

Allocated to LT garages: Battersea, Streatham.

RV 9403 Leyland Titan TD1 32seat Cravens *
* Converted double deck body with top deck removed

Wayfarer Coaches
73 Shooters Hill Road, Greenwich, SE3

Garage: At address above

Allocated to LT garages: Plumstead.

VA 8956 Leyland Tiger TS1 32seat Midland *
ORE 651 Leyland Tiger TS1 29seat E.C.O.C.
* Formerly ran with J. M. Motors (q.v.)

White Line Coaches
R. F. Knight, 321A High Road, Wood Green, N22

Garage: 737/9 Lordship Lane, Wood Green, N22

Allocated to LT garage: Muswell Hill.

UF 6928 Leyland Tiger TS2 32seat Park Royal
LMG 650 Bedford OB 32seat Duple

White Star Transport Ltd
see Blue and White Star Transport Co. Ltd

Wiggs & Son Ltd
see Grey Coaches

Windsorian
R. Try, Windsor, Berks

Garage: Windsor

Allocated to LT garage: Windsor.

RX 8569 Dennis Arrow 31seat *Body not confirmed*
VA 8959 Leyland Tiger TS1 ?seat *Body not confirmed*
CMO 493 Bedford OWB ? ?seat *Body not confirmed*
CMO 494 Bedford OWB ? ?seat *Body not confirmed*
CMO 495 Bedford OWB 28seat *Body not confirmed*
CMO 496 Bedford OWB ? ?seat *Body not confirmed*
DMO 240 Dennis Lancet III 33seat Duple
DMO 241 Dennis Lancet III 33seat Duple
DMO 243 Dennis Lancet III 33seat Duple
DMO 244 Dennis Lancet III 33seat Duple
DMO 250 Bedford OB ?seat Duple

Winfield's Coaches
H. W. Winfield, 29 Buxton Lane, Upper Caterham, Surrey

Garage: 3 Eccleston Place, Victoria, SW1

Allocated to LT garage: Victoria.

CK 4336 Leyland Tiger TS2 32seat Duple
LML 513 Bedford OWB 28seat Duple

Winwood Coaches Ltd
543 Lea Bridge Road, Leyton, E10

Garage: At address above

Allocated to LT garage: Leyton.

EV	4952	Gilford 168OT	32seat *Body not confirmed*
EYF	862	Bedford WTB1	26seat Duple
MMP	578	Bedford OB	29seat Duple
MMP	579	Bedford OB	29seat Duple

Woodside Coaches
T. J. Hutchinson
3 Woodside Way, Croydon

Garage: South Norwood Motors, Brocklesby Rd, South Norwood, SE25

Allocated to LT garages: Elmers End, Norwood.

DUK	844	AEC Regal	32seat E.C.O.C.
FRK	443	Bedford OB	27seat Duple
GVB	837	Crossley SD42	33seat Whitson

Wordsworth, J
see Dix Luxury Coaches

Worsley, C. J.
see Sunbeam

Wright Bros (London) Ltd
Cumfilery Coaches, 185 Uxbridge Road, Hanwell, W7

Garage: Edinburgh Garage, Edinburgh Road, Hanwell, W7

Allocated to LT garages: Alperton, Hanwell.

GN	4418	AEC Regal	33seat Mulliner
EXA	63	Dennis Lancet II	33seat Duple *
HMX	987	AEC Regal	32seat Strachan
MHX	321	AEC Regal	35seat Strachan
MME	364	Commer Commando	32seat Strachan
MMH	234	Commer Commando	32seat Strachan
MMY	114	AEC Regal	35seat Strachan
MMY	370	AEC Regal	35seat Strachan
OMY	502	AEC Regal	35seat Whitson
OMY	533	Maudslay Marathon III	35seat Whitson
SME	9	Bedford OB	27seat Whitson
SME	291	Commer Commando	31seat Whitson
SME	292	Commer Commando	31seat Whitson
SME	293	Commer Commando	31seat Whitson
SMF	316	Commer Commando	31seat Strachan
SMF	317	Commer Commando	31seat Strachan
SML	199	Maudslay Marathon III	33seat Whitson
SMY	253	AEC Regal III	35seat Strachan
SMY	256	Bedford OB	29seat Whitson
SMY	257	Bedford OB	29seat Whitson
TMG	167	Bedford OB	29seat Strachan
TMG	168	Bedford OB	29seat Strachan
TMG	198	Maudslay Marathon III	35seat Whitson
VML	2	Bedford OB	29seat Duple

* *later ran for J. M. Motors (q.v.)*

Coaches by Registration

Registration	Chassis	Body	Seating	Company Name
AG 4145	Leyland Tiger TS1	Brush	32	Valliant Direct Motor Coaches Ltd
AG 4152	Leyland Tiger TS1	Wadham	32	Ivanhoe Coaches
AG 6212	Tilling Stevens B10C2	Burlingham	31	D & R Motor Company
AG 6216	Tilling Stevens B10A2	Brush	31	D & R Motor Company
AG 6505	AEC Regal	Mains	32	Superior Coaches Ltd
AV 6486	Albion Valkyrie PW67	Walker (Aberdeen)	32	Rayner's Coachways Ltd
BU 6465	Leyland Tiger TS2	?	32	Lansdowne Luxury Coaches Ltd
BU 7180	Leyland Tiger TS4	?	32	Graves, G. F. & Son
BU 9450	Leyland Tiger TS7	Duple	35	Viney's Luxury Coaches
BV 4454	Leyland Tiger TS7	Duple	32	Cronshaw, Lewis Ltd
BV 5740	Tilling Stevens	Duple	32	Clifton & Kalber
BV 5741	Tilling Stevens	Duple	32	Curtis & Hearn
BV 7038	Leyland Tiger TS7	Duple	32	Cronshaw, Lewis Ltd
CK 3961	Leyland Tiger TS1	Alexander	32	J. M. Motors
CK 4107	Leyland Tiger TS1	Leyland	32	J. M. Motors
CK 4195	Leyland Tiger TS1	Harrington	32	United Service Transport Co. Ltd
CK 4292	Leyland Tiger TS2	Leyland	32	McCormack, R.
CK 4336	Leyland Tiger TS2	Duple	32	Winfield's Coaches
CK 4728	Leyland Tiger TS6	Leyland	31	Careford's Coaches
CK 4739	Leyland Tiger TS6	English Electric	32	McCormack, R.
CK 4746	Leyland Tiger TS6	English Electric	35	Banfield, Charles W.
CS 112	Gilford Hera 176SD	Wycombe	32	Clark's Red Coaches
CS 117	Gilford Hera 176SD	Wycombe	32	Paddington Transport Services Ltd
CS 1998	Albion ValkyrieSPPW69	Scottish Aviation	31	Merry's Luxury Coaches
CS 3352	Leyland Cheetah	Alexander	33	Smith's Luxury Coaches
CS 3356	Leyland Cheetah	Alexander	35	Ansell's Coaches
CS 3359	Leyland Cheetah	Alexander	37	Ansell's Coaches
CS 3370	Leyland Cheetah	Alexander	33	Smith's Luxury Coaches
CS 3372	Leyland Cheetah LZ2	Alexander	32	Paddington Transport Services Ltd
CS 3375	Leyland Cheetah	Alexander	37	Ansell's Coaches
DB 5234	Tilling Stevens B10A2	E.C.O.C.	31	Ansell's Coaches
DB 9384	Tilling Stevens B10AZ	E.C.O.C.	31	Overland Lismore Coaches Ltd
DB 9487	Leyland Tiger TS4	Harrington	33	Elms, Longman Motor Services Ltd
DF 8186	Leyland Tiger TS2	London Lorries	32	Empress Coaches
DF 8901	Guy	E.C.O.C.	32	Halpin, T. W.
DF 8902	Guy	Beadle	30	Jays Coaches
DF 8904	Guy	E.C.O.C.	32	Halpin, T. W.
DM 9308	Thornycroft Cygnet	Thurgood	32	Safeway Coaches
DR 4785	Leyland Lion PLSC	Mumford	33	D & R Motor Company
DX 8047	Tilling Stevens B10A2	?	35	Omnia Transporters Ltd
DX 8049	Tilling Stevens B10A2	?	35	Omnia Transporters Ltd
DX 8092	Tilling Stevens B10A2	?	35	Omnia Transporters Ltd
DX 8590	Tilling Stevens B10A2	?	32	Omnia Transporters Ltd
DY 8062	AEC Regal	Harrington	32	Camden Coaches Ltd
EA 8300	Leyland Tiger TS7	Duple	32	United Service Transport Co. Ltd
EB 9897	Dennis Lancet	Willowbrook	32	J. M. Motors
EN 6580	Dennis Lancet II	Dennis	32	Empress Motors Ltd
ER 8886	Leyland Lion PLSC3	E.C.O.C.	34	Omnia Transporters Ltd
EV 423	Maudslay ML3E	London Lorries ?	32	Classique Coaches Ltd
EV 424	Maudslay ML3E	London Lorries ?	32	Classique Coaches Ltd
EV 942	Maudslay ML3E	London Lorries ?	32	Classique Coaches Ltd
EV 943	Maudslay ML3E	London Lorries ?	32	Classique Coaches Ltd
EV 1266	Leyland Tiger TS4	London Lorries	32	Banfield, Charles W.

EV	1780	AEC Regal	Duple	32	United Service Transport Co. Ltd
EV	4952	Gilford 168OT	?	32	Winwood Coaches Ltd
EV	6264	Leyland Tiger TS4	Petty	32	Horseshoe Coaches
EX	4360	Tilling Stevens	Watson	35	Grey Coaches
FA	5849	Guy Arab	Brush	34	Radio Coaches
FA	5855	Guy Arab	Brush	34	Radio Coaches
FG	6110	Daimler CF6	Duple	32	Henry Saloon Coaches Ltd
FJ	9061	Dennis Lancet	Duple	31	Acorn Motors Ltd
FM	4504	Daimler CF6	Duple	32	Henry Saloon Coaches Ltd
FS	6007	Daimler CP6	Burlingham	32	Surrell, L. D., Ltd
FS	6008	Daimler CP6	Burlingham	32	Red Line Continental Motorways
FV	49	Leyland Tiger TS1	Duple	33	Viney's Luxury Coaches
FV	448	AEC Daimler CF6*	Duple	33	Margo's *with an AEC radiator.*
FV	972	Tilling Stevens B10A2	Burlingham	36	Ansell's Coaches
FV	5591	Leyland Tiger TS6	Burlingham	32	McCormack, R.
GC	7407	AEC Regal	Duple	32	United Service Transport Co. Ltd
GF	547	AEC Regal	Thurgood	35	Premier Omnibus Company
GF	581	AEC Regal	Thurgood	35	Premier Omnibus Company
GF	595	AEC Regal	? (rebodied)	32	Elms, Longman Motor Services Ltd
GF	597	AEC Regal	Wadham	32	Broadway Coaches
GF	1737	AEC Regal	Harrington	32	Grundon, W. E.
GF	5126	AEC Regal	Duple	32	United Service Transport Co. Ltd
GF	5249	AEC Regal	Beadle	32	Black & White Coaches Ltd
GH	623	AEC Regal 1	Burlingham	32	Shirley Coaches
GH	3802	AEC Regal	Ransomes	32	Davis, L. C. & Sons
GH	3817	AEC Regal	Short	33	Sunbeam
GH	3827	AEC Regal	Duple	32	Golden Star Coaches Ltd
GH	3828	AEC Regal	Ransomes (?)	32	Black & White Coaches Ltd
GJ	8071	AEC Regal	Duple	32	United Service Transport Co. Ltd
GK	3411	Gilford 168OT	Wycombe	31	Twigg, S. V.
GK	8612	Gilford 168OT	Abbott	28	Emerald Coaches Ltd
GN	1368	AEC Regal	Harrington	33	Atkins, Fred G.
GN	1376	AEC Regal	Harrington	33	Atkins, Fred G.
GN	1378	AEC Regal	Harrington	32	Bexleyheath Transport Co. Ltd
GN	4417	AEC Regal	E.C.O.C.	33	Sunbeam
GN	4418	AEC Regal	Mulliner	33	Wright Bros (London) Ltd
GN	9571	AEC Regal	Hoyal	33	Elms, Longman Motor Services Ltd
GN	9745	AEC Regal	Hoyal	32	Ranelagh Coaches
GO	1044	Leyland Tiger TS1	?	32	Fleet Coaches
GP	3380	Leyland Tiger TS1	Harrington	32	Monico Motorways
				also	Hall Brothers
GU	3695	AEC Reliance	Duple	33	Rayner's Coachways Ltd
GV	411	Leyland Tiger TS	Petty	32	Argosy Super Coaches
GW	644	Leyland Tiger TS4	Harrington	31	Grey Green Coaches
GW	646	Leyland Tiger TS4	Harrington	31	Grey Green Coaches
GW	649	Leyland Tiger TS4	Harrington	32	Ansell's Coaches
GW	2008	Gilford 168OT	Wycombe	32	Champion Coaches
GX	166	AEC Regal	Duple	32	Lansdowne Luxury Coaches Ltd
GZ	728	Leyland Cheetah LZ	?	33	Hall Brothers
GZ	729	Leyland Cheetah	Duple	31	Rayner's Coachways Ltd
HD	3440	Leyland Tiger TS1	Weymann	31	Ansell's Coaches
HG	1024	AEC Regent	Roe	50	Lansdowne Luxury Coaches Ltd
HG	1223	AEC Regent	Brush	50	Lansdowne Luxury Coaches Ltd
HV	1184	Tilling Stevens	Beadle	32	Elms, Longman Motor Services Ltd
HV	1967	AEC Regal	Barking Garage & Engineering Co. Ltd	32	Ranelagh Coaches
HV	2751	AEC Regal	Park Royal	32	Battens Coaches Ltd
				also	Bontonian Coaches
HV	2752	AEC Regal	Park Royal	35	Battens Coaches Ltd
HV	2753	AEC Regal	Park Royal	32	Battens Coaches Ltd
JA	8865	Bedford WTB	?	25	Argosy Super Coaches
JD	1167	AEC Regal	Strachan	32	Grundon, W. E.
JD	1378	AEC Regal	Strachan	32	Julius and Lockwood
JD	9253	AEC Regal	Strachan	33	Clarke's Luxury Coaches
JF	2779	Dennis Lancet 1	Duple	32	Cosy Coaches
JG	1442	Tilling Stevens B49CZ	Hoyal	35	Bexleyheath Transport Co. Ltd

JG	5448	Leyland Tiger TS7	Park Royal	32	Broadway Coaches
JG	6524	Leyland Tiger TS7	Park Royal	32	Monico Motorways
JJ	8824	Leyland Tiger TS4	Harrington	33	Graves, G. F. & Son
JT	4745	Commer	?	25	Elms Coaches
JW	2744	Maudslay ML3	?	32	Hall Brothers
JW	4901	Maudslay ML3	Burlingham	32	Hall Brothers
JX	5264	AEC Regent	Park Royal	56	Lansdowne Luxury Coaches Ltd
JX	5395	Leyland Cheetah		?	Alexandra Coaches
JX	6427	AEC Regent	Park Royal	56	Lansdowne Luxury Coaches Ltd
KJ	1612	TSM C60AT	Beadle	31	Mountain Transport Services Ltd
KJ	1863	Commer Invader	Chatham Motor Co.	20	Roberts & Dickenson
KJ	1968	AEC Regal	Santus	33	Enterprise Coaches
KJ	2376	Leyland Tiger TS2	Short	32	Banfield, Charles W.
KJ	2914	Tilling Stevens C60A7	Roberts	32	Grey Coaches
KJ	5432	Leyland Tiger TS3	Short	32	Banfield, Charles W.
KJ	5440	Leyland Tiger TS4	Short	32	Banfield, Charles W.
KJ	6981	Thornycroft Cygnet	Strachan	32	Parkside Coaches
KJ	7440	Leyland Tiger TS2	Short	31	J. M. Motors
KP	3053	Tilling Stevens B10	Harrington	31	Grey Coaches
KP	8372	Leyland Lion LT1	Ransomes	32	Radio Coaches
KR	1744	Leyland Tiger TS2	Short	32	Roberts & Dickenson
KR	9207	Morris Viceroy	Harrington	25	Star Luxury Coaches
KX	8092	Dennis Lancet	Duple	32	Acorn Motors Ltd
KX	8644	AEC Regal	Duple	33	Clarke's Luxury Coaches
				also	Overland Lismore Coaches Ltd
MG	7867	Commer Commando	Thurgood	33	Hampton Coaches
MS	8666	Leyland Tiger TS1	Alexander	32	Feltham Transport Co.
MS	8828	Leyland Tiger TS1	Alexander	32	Feltham Transport Co.
MS	8834	Leyland Tiger TS1	Alexander	32	Feltham Transport Co.
MS	9020	Leyland Tiger TS1	Alexander	33	Harrison and Hole
MS	9061	Leyland Lion LT1	Alexander	32	Roberts & Dickenson
MV	2592	Daimler CF6	?	32	Grove Coaches
MV	2668	Leyland Tiger TS4	Duple	32	Lewis, C. G.
NV	3778	Maudslay ML3	Spite	32	Cowell, W.
OW	3434	Thornycroft Daring	Park Royal	56	Safeway Coaches
OY	2568	Leyland Tiger TS4	Harrington	33	Bennett, John (Croydon) Ltd
OY	2569	Leyland Tiger TS4	Harrington	32	Bennett, John (Croydon) Ltd
OY	2570	Leyland Tiger TS4	Harrington	33	Bennett, John (Croydon) Ltd
OY	2574	Leyland Tiger TS4	Harrington	32	Bennett, John (Croydon) Ltd
OY	2577	Leyland Tiger TS4	Harrington	32	Bennett, John (Croydon) Ltd
PG	7025	AEC Regal	Strachan	32	Bontonian Coaches
PG	9575	Gilford 168OT	Metcalfe	33	Champion Coaches
PJ	3827	AEC Regal	Burlingham	35	Roberts & Dickenson
PL	5879	Gilford AS6	Duple	20	Golden Miller Coaches
PV	4636	Leyland Lion LT8	Duple	35	Valliant Direct Motor Coaches Ltd
RC	408	SOS IM4	Brush	32	Mountain Transport Services Ltd
RC	409	SOS IM4	Brush	32	Mountain Transport Services Ltd
RC	410	SOS IM4	Brush	32	Mountain Transport Services Ltd
RC	426	SOS IM4	Brush	32	Mountain Transport Services Ltd
RN	8859	Leyland Tiger	Duple	33	McCormack, R.
RV	1492	Tilling Stevens B10A2	Park Royal	32	Grove Coaches
RV	1495	Tilling Stevens B10AZ	Park Royal	32	Parker's Coaches (Kingsbury)
RV	9403	Leyland Titan TD1	Cravens (*single deck*)	32	Watkins, W.
RX	8569	Dennis Arrow	?	?	Windsorian
SC	4374	Leyland Tiger TS2	Duple	32	Banfield, Charles W.
SC	4376	Leyland Tiger TS2	Duple	32	Banfield, Charles W.
TE	5711	Leyland Tiger TS2	Leyland	32	Argosy Super Coaches
TG	1152	AEC Regal	Metcalfe	35	Radio Coaches
TH	3580	Leyland Tiger TS6	Duple	33	Henry Saloon Coaches Ltd
TS	8420	Leyland Lion	?	?	Hearn, P.
TX	9498	AEC Regal	Burlingham	35	Roberts & Dickenson
UF	5807	Leyland Tiger TS2	Park Royal	32	Clark's Red Coaches
UF	6928	Leyland Tiger TS2	Park Royal	32	White Line Coaches
UF	8833	Leyland Tiger TS4	Strachan	33	Graves, G. F. & Son
UF	8834	Leyland Tiger TS4	Harrington	31	Roberts & Dickenson
UF	8840	Leyland Tiger TS4	Harrington	32	Henry Saloon Coaches Ltd

UF 8843	Leyland Tiger TS4	Harrington	33	Graves, G. F. & Son
UK 8450	AEC Regal	Burlingham	31	Lucky Line Coaches Ltd
UN 187	Daimler CF6	Duple	32	Henry Saloon Coaches Ltd
UR 6802	AEC Regal	Harrington	32	Paddington Transport Services Ltd
UR 6895	AEC Regal	Thurgood	35	Premier Omnibus Company
UR 9535	AEC Regal	Petty	32	Avondale Safety Coaches
UU 9161	AEC Regent*	(*single deck*)	32	Cosy Coaches
	* with Leyland radiator.			
UU 9342	AEC Reliance	Beadle	32	Castle Coaches
UW 8773	AEC Regal	Beadle	33	Grundon, W. E.
UW 8901	Leyland Tiger TS2	Duple	33	Grey Green Coaches
UW 8905	Leyland Tiger TS2	Duple	33	Grey Green Coaches
VA 8890	Leyland Tiger TS1	Midland	32	Valliant Direct Motor Coaches Ltd
VA 8956	Leyland Tiger TS1	Midland	32	J. M. Motors
			also	Wayfarer Coaches
VA 8959	Leyland Tiger TS1	?	?	Windsorian
VD 4449	Leyland Tiger TS7	Leyland	39	Lewis, C. G.
VE 306	Leyland Lion PLSC3	E.C.O.C.	33	Omnia Transporters Ltd
VH 6530	AEC Regal	Brush	32	Roberts & Dickenson
VH 7535	AEC Regal	Park Royal	32	Enterprise Coaches
VN 7172	Albion PV	?	31	Majestic Luxury Coaches Ltd
VP 9531	Maudslay ML6A	Buckingham	32	Rayner's Coachways Ltd
VS 2094	AEC Regal	Harrington	32	Julius and Lockwood
VT 7140	Tilling Stevens B10A2	Lauton	32	Ansell's Coaches
VU 425	AEC Regal	?	32	Premier Omnibus Company
VX 7851	Gilford 168SD	Duple	26	Cowell, W.
WG 333	Gilford 168OT	Wycombe	32	Topple's Coaches
WG 1274	Gilford 168OT	Wycombe	32	Horseshoe Coaches
WG 1276	Gilford 168OT	Wycombe	32	Elms, Phillips & Brown
WG 1283	Gilford 168OT	Wycombe	29	Ideal Safety Coaches
WG 2310	Gilford Hera L176S	Wycombe	32	Feltham Transport Co.
WG 2314	Gilford Hera L176S	Wycombe	32	Ranelagh Coaches
WG 4547	Bedford WTB	?	?	Careford's Coaches
WH 1299	Leyland Tiger TS1	Harrington	32	London Road Coaches
WH 3787	Leyland Tiger TS4	Spicer	32	Grosvenor Coaches Ltd
WH 8650	AEC Regal	Watson	32	Davis, L. C. & Sons
WJ 6505	Leyland Tiger TS4	Cravens	32	Eastern Belle Motor Coaches Ltd,
WJ 7173	Leyland Tiger TS4	Cravens	32	Gidea Park Coaches Ltd
WJ 7175	Leyland Tiger TS4	Cravens	32	Gidea Park Coaches Ltd
WN 4370	Leyland Tiger TS4	Harrington or Beadle	32	Empress Coaches
WN 4767	AEC Regent	Beadle (*single deck*)	32	Superior Coaches Ltd
WN 4869	AEC Regent	Harrington (*single deck*)	32	Davis, L. C. & Sons
WN 8634	Tilling Stevens	?	32	Grey Coaches
WN 9380	Dennis Lancet II	Andrews	32	Clifton & Kalber
			also	Dryer's Coaches Ltd
WN 9804	Leyland Lion LT7	Duple	32	Valliant Direct Motor Coaches Ltd
WS 8001	Leyland Cheetah	Alexander	33	Smith's Luxury Coaches
WS 8007	Leyland Cheetah	Alexander	33	Smith's Luxury Coaches
WS 8009	Leyland Cheetah	Duple	32	Hearn, P.
WS 8011	Leyland Cheetah	Alexander	32	Hearn, P.
WS 8014	Leyland Cheetah	Alexander	33	Smith's Luxury Coaches
WS 8018	Leyland Cheetah	Alexander	33	Smith's Luxury Coaches
WS 8019	Leyland Cheetah	Alexander	33	Smith's Luxury Coaches
WS 8020	Leyland Cheetah LZ2	Alexander	36	Castle Coaches
WS 8022	Leyland Cheetah	Alexander	33	Smith's Luxury Coaches
WS 8025	Leyland Cheetah	Alexander	33	Smith's Luxury Coaches
WS 8027	Leyland Cheetah	Alexander	33	Smith's Luxury Coaches
WS 8029	Leyland Cheetah	Alexander	33	Smith's Luxury Coaches
WS 8036	Leyland Cheetah	Alexander	33	Smith's Luxury Coaches
WS 8045	Leyland Cheetah	Alexander	33	Smith's Luxury Coaches
WV 9633	Bedford WTL	?	25	Hearn, P.
WX 2119	Tilling Stevens B10A2	Roe	32	Grey Coaches
WX 2142	Tilling Stevens B10A2	United	32	Grey Coaches
WX 8989	Tilling Stevens B49A7	E.C.O.C.	32	Sydenham Coaches
XJ 1085	Tilling Stevens B39A4	Duple ?	32	Progress Coaches
XS 2823	Albion Viking	Duple	32	Carter's

XS	4407	Albion Valkyrie 3 axle	Cowieson	39	Avonley Coaches
XS	4765	Albion Valkyrie 3 axle	Cowieson	39	Ansell's Coaches
XS	5110	Albion Valkyrie CX11	Cowieson	35	Avonley Coaches
YF	1906	Tilling Stevens B9A	?	36	Omnia Transporters Ltd
YG	1706	AEC Regal	Burlingham	33	Sydenham Coaches
YS	4488	Albion Valkyrie PW69	Cowieson	35	Ansell's Coaches
AAL	159	Leyland Cub	?	26	Sunbeam
ABH	307	AEC Regal	Strachan	32	Black & White Coaches Ltd
ACJ	434	Bedford WTB	Duple	26	Radio Coaches
ADL	539	Dennis Lancet	?	33	Boughton's Coaches Ltd
AGF	928	AEC Regal	Strachan	32	Ideal Safety Coaches
AGH	297	Leyland Tiger TS4	Harrington	32	Black & White Coaches Ltd
AGH	298	Leyland Tiger TS4	Harrington	32	Black & White Coaches Ltd
AGJ	614	AEC Regal	Short	32	Julius and Lockwood
AGP	494	Albion Valiant	Duple	32	Pearl and Gunn
AHR	647	Leyland Cub	Weymann	20	Safeway Coaches
AJD	538	Bedford OWB	Duple	29	Battens Coaches Ltd
AJW	871	AEC Regal	Strachan	32	Garner's Coaches Ltd
AKL	472	Dennis Lancet	Duple	31	Acorn Motors Ltd
AKL	667	Commer Centaur	Harrington	20	Roberts & Dickenson
ALM	266	AEC Regal	Duple	32	Carshalton & Wallington Coaches
AND	846	Leyland Tiger TS4	Duple	33	Leighton Coach Co. Ltd
ANO	345	Tilling Stevens	Duple	32	Bickley Coaches
ANP	611	Maudslay ML3	Mulliner	32	Green Luxury Coaches
ARK	568	Dennis Lancet	Harrington	32	Bexleyheath Transport Co. Ltd
ARR	829	AEC 'Q'	Cravens	32	Broadway Coaches
AUP	429	Dennis Lancet II	?	32	Davis, Fred & Sons
AUX	776	Bedford WTB	Duple	26	Halpin, T. W.
AUX	891	Bedford WTB	Duple	28	Radio Coaches
AWJ	232	AEC Ranger	Cravens	29	Sunbeam
AWJ	234	AEC Ranger	Cravens	29	Sunbeam
AXK	845	AEC Regal	Harrington	32	London Road Coaches
AXO	518	Dennis Lancet	Duple	29	Empress Motors Ltd
AYE	388	AEC Regal	Strachan	32	Avondale Safety Coaches
AYH	93	Maudslay ML3	Duple	32	Eastern Belle Motor Coaches Ltd,
AYH	297	Leyland Lion LT5A	Birch	35	Knowler's Coaches Ltd
AYH	350	Maudslay ML3	Duple	32	Rayner's Coachways Ltd
AYV	717	Leyland Cub	LPTB	20	J. M. Motors
				also	Overland Lismore Coaches Ltd
BAB	799	Maudslay ML5B	Grose	33	Parkside Coaches
BBV	418	Daimler CVD6	Duple	35	Cronshaw, Lewis Ltd
BBV	419	Daimler CVD6	Duple	35	Cronshaw, Lewis Ltd
BBV	622	Dennis Lancet III	Duple	35	Cronshaw, Lewis Ltd
BBV	623	Dennis Lancet III	Duple	35	Cronshaw, Lewis Ltd
BBV	656	Daimler CVD6	Duple	35	Cronshaw, Lewis Ltd
BCB	7	Bedford OB	Duple	29	Cronshaw, Lewis Ltd
BCB	143	Daimler CVD6	Duple	35	Cronshaw, Lewis Ltd
BCB	477	Dennis Lancet III	Duple	35	Cronshaw, Lewis Ltd
BCB	684	Bedford OB	Duple	29	Cronshaw, Lewis Ltd
BCJ	620	Bedford WTB	Duple	26	Currie, P. Ltd
BHJ	676	AEC Regal	Harrington	32	Progress Coaches
BHR	138	?	?	26	Topple's Coaches
BHV	792	Bedford OB	Duple	29	Lacey's (East Ham) Ltd
BHV	793	Bedford OB	Duple	29	Lacey's (East Ham) Ltd
BJD	815	Bedford OB	Duple	29	Clark's Red Coaches
BKT	602	AEC Regal	Duple	32	Bookham Saloons
BLO	901	Gilford Hera 176S	Wycombe	32	Davis, Fred & Sons
BLY	106	Leyland Tiger TS6	Harrington	32	Grey Green Coaches
BLY	667	Leyland Tiger TS6	Duple	32	Grey Green Coaches
BMG	101	Leyland Lion LT5A	Beadle	32	Usher's Saloon Coaches
BPX	733	Bedford WTB	Duple	25	Eastern Belle Motor Coaches Ltd,
BRE	338	Dennis Lancet	?	32	Boughton's Coaches Ltd
BRK	477	Dennis Lancet II	Harrington	32	Graves, G. F. & Son
BRO	420	AEC Regal	Duple	32	Lee's Luxury Coaches Ltd
BUC	580	Leyland Tiger TS6	Harrington	32	Grey Green Coaches
BUX	771	Bedford OWB	Mulliner	28	Harold Wood Coach Services

BWM 552	Albion Victor	?	26	Topple's Coaches
BXH 126	Thornycroft Cygnet	Thurgood	32	Streatham Vale Luxury Coaches
BXH 678	Dennis Lancet 1	?	32	Harrison and Hole
BXH 778	Dennis Lancet 1	?	32	Thorne Bros.
BXK 78	Bedford WTL	Duple	26	Classique Coaches Ltd
BXN 426	AEC Regal	Harrington	32	London Road Coaches
BXO 209	AEC Regal	Harrington	32	Carter's
BXV 335	Leyland Titan TD1	? (*single deck*)	32	Clark's Red Coaches
CAN 155	Bedford OB	Duple	29	Clark's Red Coaches
CAN 260	Bedford OB	Duple	29	Clark's Red Coaches
CAW 885	Bedford OWB	Duple	28	Boughton's Coaches Ltd
CBA 765	Leyland PS1	Burlingham	33	Banfield, Charles W.
CBA 766	AEC Regal	Plaxton	33	Ranelagh Coaches
CBE 616	Bedford OWB	Duple	32	London Road Coaches
CCD 727	Leyland Tiger TS7	Harrington	32	Valliant Direct Motor Coaches Ltd
CCD 750	Leyland Tiger TS7	Harrington	32	Valliant Direct Motor Coaches Ltd
CCG 229	Ford V8	?	20	Star Luxury Coaches
CEL 326	Bedford WTB	Duple	25	Gatehouse Coaches
CHM 132	AEC Regal	Thurgood	35	Battens Coaches Ltd
CHM 708	Dennis Lancet III	Duple	35	Broadway Coaches
CHV 518	Daimler CVD6	Thurgood	35	Battens Coaches Ltd
CJD 596	Bedford OYD	Bonallack	29	Mountain Transport Services Ltd
CLA 933	Maudslay ML5	Duple	35	Ansell's Coaches
CLC 695	Leyland Tiger TS7	Duple	32	United Service Transport Co. Ltd
CLY 18	Leyland Tiger TS7	Harrington	33	Atkins, Fred G.
CMH 775	Leyland Tiger TS7	Duple	32	Valliant Direct Motor Coaches Ltd
CML 839	Bedford WTL	Thurgood	25	Modern Super Coaches
CMO 493	?	?	?	Windsorian
CMO 494	?	?	?	Windsorian
CMO 495	Bedford OWB	?	28	Windsorian
CMO 496	?	?	?	Windsorian
CMO 498	Bedford OWB	Mulliner	28	Foster's Luxury Coaches
CNJ 347	Bedford OWB	Duple	27	Sargent, H. J.
CNJ 887	Bedford OWB	Duple	27	Sargent, H. J.
CNN 865	Leyland Lion LT7	Duple	39	Bexleyheath Transport Co. Ltd
CNO 30	Tilling Stevens	Duple	31	Black & White Coaches Ltd
CNO 75	Gilford Hera 176S	Wycombe	29	Roberts & Dickenson
CNO 76	Gilford Hera 176S	Wycombe	29	Roberts & Dickenson
CPH 230	Thornycroft Cygnet	Thurgood	32	Streatham Vale Luxury Coaches
CPJ 122	Maudslay SF40	Duple	35	A and W Omnibus Co. Ltd
CPM 121	Bedford OWB	Duple	27	Sargent, H. J.
CRD 585	Leyland Tiger TS7	Burlingham	33	Smith's Luxury Coaches
CRK 441	Dennis Lancet II	Harrington	32	Bourne & Balmer (Croydon) Ltd
CRR 820	Leyland Cub	Brush	23	Kilsby, N. J. & K. B.
CUC 104	Bedford WTB	?	26	J. M. Motors
CUC 770	Maudslay ML5	Duple	32	Ansell's Coaches
CUL 65	Tilling Stevens HA39	Duple	32	Grey Coaches
CUW 334	Dennis Ace	Dennis	24	Elms, Longman Motor Services Ltd
CUW 802	Leyland Tiger TS7	Harrington	32	Grey Green Coaches
CVH 240	Bedford OB	Duple	29	Golden Miller Coaches
CVH 317	Bedford OB	Roberts (Huddersfield)	29	Emerald Coaches Ltd
CXM 711	Leyland Tiger TS7	Strachan	21	Red Line Continental Motorways
CXT 416	Leyland Tiger TS7	Harrington	32	Grey Green Coaches
CXT 536	Dennis Lancet II	Metcalfe	32	Gilbert's Luxury Coaches Ltd
CXT 690	Dennis Lancet II	Duple	33	Popular Coaches Ltd
CXW 364	Dennis Lancet II	Duple	32	Empress Coaches
CYL 216	Dennis Lancet	Dennis	33	Thorne Bros.
CYL 853	Dennis Lancet II	Metcalfe	32	Gilbert's Luxury Coaches Ltd
CYY 308	Dennis Lancet II	Duple	35	Harold Wood Coach Services
DAU 453	AEC Regal	Cravens	32	Black & White Coaches Ltd
DAW 994	Commer Commando	Harrington	30	J. M. Motors
DEL 102	Bedford WTB	Duple	25	Emerald Coaches Ltd
DGG 892	Bedford OWB	Duple	28	Banfield, Charles W.
DGK 673	Leyland Cub	Duple	26	Advance Motor Services
DHR 24	Bedford OWB	Duple	28	Carshalton & Wallington Coaches
DKB 809	Leyland Cheetah	?	32	Radio Coaches

DKK	677	Dennis Lancet II	Duple	32	Bexleyheath Transport Co. Ltd
DLT	11	Bedford WTB	Duple	25	Progress Coaches
DLX	912	Leyland Tiger TS7	Duple	32	Lewis, C. G.
DLX	913	Leyland Tiger TS7	Duple	33	Lewis, C. G.
DLY	984	Dennis Lancet II	Duple	33	Empress Motors Ltd
DMO	240	Dennis	?	?	Windsorian
DMO	241	Dennis Lancet III	Duple	33	Windsorian
DMO	243	Dennis Lancet III	Duple	33	Windsorian
DMO	244	Dennis Lancet III	Duple	33	Windsorian
DMO	250	Bedford OB	Duple	?	Windsorian
DMX	3	Dennis Lancet II	Duple	33	Harold Wood Coach Services
DMX	198	Leyland Tiger TS7	Duple	32	Venture Transport (Hendon) Ltd
DNO	724	Ford	?	27	Radio Coaches
DNT	90	Bedford OB	Mulliner	28	Monico Motorways
DOX	601	Leyland Lion LT8	Burlingham	35	Radio Coaches
DPD	859	Dennis Ace	Dennis	20	Dagenham Coach Services
DPL	448	Dennis Lancet	Strachan	33	Thorpe Coaches Ltd
DPU	90	AEC Regal	Duple	32	Davis, L. C. & Sons
DPU	648	Bedford WTB	Duple	26	Ferndale Coaches
DRK	51	Dennis Lancet II	Harrington	32	Bourne & Balmer (Croydon) Ltd
DRK	52	Dennis Lancet II	Harrington	32	Bourne & Balmer (Croydon) Ltd
DRO	179	AEC Regal	Duple	32	Lee's Luxury Coaches Ltd
DTO	15	Leyland Cub	Duple	25	Currie, P. Ltd
DUK	844	AEC Regal	E.C.O.C.	32	Woodside Coaches
DUS	486	Bedford OWB	Duple	28	Cosy Coaches
DUU	713	Leyland Tiger TS7	Duple	32	Ferndale Coaches
DUU	715	Leyland Lion LT7	?	35	Cosy Coaches
DXD	784	Bedford WTB	Duple	25	Julius and Lockwood
DXF	582	Dennis Lancet II	Strachan	32	Garner's Coaches Ltd
DXF	583	Dennis Lancet II	Strachan	32	Garner's Coaches Ltd
DXF	584	Dennis Lancet II	Strachan	32	Garner's Coaches Ltd
DXF	585	Dennis Lancet II	Strachan	32	Garner's Coaches Ltd
DXF	586	Dennis Lancet II	Strachan	32	Garner's Coaches Ltd
DXF	587	Dennis Lancet II	Strachan	32	Avondale Safety Coaches
DXF	612	Tilling Stevens HA39A7	Duple	32	Grey Coaches
DXL	610	Dennis Lancet II	Burlingham	32	Grey Coaches
DXT	595	Leyland Tiger TS7	Strachan ?	32	Valliant Direct Motor Coaches Ltd
DXV	375	Leyland Tiger TS7	Harrington	33	Grey Green Coaches
DXV	376	Leyland Tiger TS7	Harrington	33	Grey Green Coaches
DXV	377	Leyland Tiger TS7	Harrington	33	Grey Green Coaches
DXV	378	Leyland Tiger TS7	Harrington	33	Grey Green Coaches
DXV	379	Leyland Tiger TS7	Harrington	33	Grey Green Coaches
DXV	882	Albion Victor	Strachan	29	Safeway Coaches
DYF	751	Bedford WTB	Duple	29	Garner's Coaches Ltd
DYF	770	Dennis Lancet II	Metcalfe	32	Camden Coaches Ltd
DYK	327	Leyland Cub	Duple	27	Advance Motor Services
DYL	904	Leyland FEC	Leyland	34	Castle Coaches
DYO	298	Leyland Tiger	Beadle	32	R.A.C.S.
DYO	375	Dennis Lancet II	Duple	33	Popular Coaches Ltd
EHO	919	Bedford OWB	Duple	32	London Road Coaches
EJB	645	Commer Commando	Allweather	30	Lucky Line Coaches Ltd
EJU	832	Maudslay Marathon III	Whitson	33	Radio Coaches
EKK	107	Dennis Lancet II	Duple	32	Bexleyheath Transport Co. Ltd
EKV	416	Commer Q4	Plaxton	30	Radio Coaches
ELP	98	Bedford WTB	Duple	26	Streatham Vale Luxury Coaches
ENM	682	Albion PH115	?	26	Radio Coaches
EOC	347	Leyland Tiger TS3	Plaxton	31	Clark's Red Coaches
EOY	337	AEC Regal	Harrington	32	Bourne & Balmer (Croydon) Ltd
EPA	161	Bedford	WTB	25	Acorn Motors Ltd
EPU	120	Tilling Stevens	Duple	32	Lansdowne Luxury Coaches Ltd
ERF	308	Dennis Lancet II	Dennis	35	Downey, J. J. & B. R.
ETW	89	Ford (FC)	Mulliner	26	Barking Coaches Ltd
				also	Halpin, T. W.
ETW	862	Bedford WTB1	Duple	25	Boughton's Coaches Ltd
ETW	863	Bedford WTB1	Metcalfe	25	Boughton's Coaches Ltd
EUM	900	Dennis Lancet II	Dennis	32	Rose Transport Co. Ltd

EUW	54	Bedford WTB	Duple	25	Streatham Vale Luxury Coaches
EWT	806	Leyland Tiger TS7	English Electric	31	Monico Motorways
EXA	63	Dennis Lancet II	Duple	33	J. M. Motors
				also	Wright Bros (London) Ltd
EXF	199	Dennis Lancet I	Dennis	32	Thorne Bros.
EXF	921	Leyland Cheetah	Harrington	32	J. M. Motors
EXH	14	Leyland Tiger TS8	Duple	33	Lewis, C. G.
EXO	345	Leyland Tiger TS8	Harrington	33	Grey Green Coaches
EXO	346	Leyland Tiger TS8	Harrington	32	Grey Green Coaches
EXO	348	Leyland Tiger TS8	Harrington	32	Grey Green Coaches
EXO	529	Morris Dictator	Duple	33	Empress Motors Ltd
EXO	530	Morris Dictator	Duple	33	Empress Motors Ltd
EXO	797	Dennis Lancet II	Duple	32	Thorpe Coaches Ltd
EXT	615	Leyland Tiger TS8	Duple	33	Lewis, C. G.
EXT	618	Leyland Tiger TS1	Duple	32	Ranelagh Coaches
EYE	592	Leyland Tiger TS1	Duple	33	Viney's Luxury Coaches
EYE	594	Leyland Titan TD1	Duple *(single deck)*	32	Cliff's Saloon Coaches Ltd
EYE	595	Leyland Titan TD1	Duple *(single deck)*	32	Cliff's Saloon Coaches Ltd
EYE	598	Leyland Tiger TS2	Harrington	32	Clark's Red Coaches
EYF	862	Bedford WTB1	Duple	26	Winwood Coaches Ltd
EYF	866	Leyland Tiger TS8	Duple	32	Valliant Direct Motor Coaches Ltd
EYF	867	Leyland Tiger TS8	Metcalfe	32	Valliant Direct Motor Coaches Ltd
EYL	862	Leyland Tiger TS7	Duple	32	Valliant Direct Motor Coaches Ltd
FDA	257	Leyland PS1	Mulliner	33	Argosy Super Coaches
FDH	430	Leyland Cub	Burlingham	26	Emerald Coaches Ltd
FEH	625	Dennis Lancet II	Willowbrook	39	Tyler, R. A.
FGT	950	Leyland Tiger TS2	Duple	32	Banfield, Charles W.
FLE	504	Bedford WTB	Duple	26	Halpin, T. W.
				also	Lacey's (East Ham) Ltd
FLE	509	Bedford WTB	Duple	26	Banfield, Charles W.
FLH	684	Leyland Tiger TS8	Harrington	33	Grey Green Coaches
FLH	685	Leyland Tiger TS8	Harrington	33	Grey Green Coaches
FMJ	44	Daimler CVD6	Yorkshire Yachtbuilders	33	Radio Coaches
FMP	56	AEC Regal	Strachan	32	Valliant Direct Motor Coaches Ltd
FMP	979	Leyland Lion LT7	Duple	35	Clifton & Kalber
FNN	669	Leyland Cheetah	Brush	32	J. M. Motors
FOR	169	Leyland PS1	Duple	33	Clark's Red Coaches
FOY	323	Bedford OB	Duple	29	Jewell's Coaches
FPE	229	Bedford WTB	Willmott	26	Graves, G. F. & Son
FRK	443	Bedford OB	Duple	27	Woodside Coaches
FRY	962	Commer Q4	Pearson	30	Star Luxury Coaches
FTT	807	Bedford OWB	Duple	28	Avonley Coaches
FUU	968	Bedford WTB	Duple	26	Banfield, Charles W.
FXR	336	Leyland Cheetah	Duple	32	A and W Omnibus Co. Ltd
GAA	872	Bedford OB	Wadham	29	Monico Motorways
GAL	596	Bedford OWB	Duple	32	Avonley Coaches
GBM	719	Daimler CVD6	Plaxton	33	Radio Coaches
GBY	85	Bedford OB	Duple	29	Bennett, John (Croydon) Ltd
GBY	128	AEC Regal I	Harrington	32	Bourne & Balmer (Croydon) Ltd
GBY	567	Bedford OB	Duple	29	Bennett, John (Croydon) Ltd
GBY	640	AEC Regal I	Harrington	32	Bourne & Balmer (Croydon) Ltd
GBY	800	Bedford OB	Duple	29	Bennett, John (Croydon) Ltd
GGC	770	Bedford OWB	Duple	32	Cream Coaches Ltd
GGC	771	Bedford OWB	Duple	32	Cream Coaches Ltd
GLH	203	Bedford OWB	Mulliner	32	Cream Coaches Ltd
GLH	204	Bedford OWB	Mulliner	32	Cream Coaches Ltd
GLU	601	Dennis Lancet	Strachan	32	Thorpe Coaches Ltd
GRK	399	AEC Regal I	Harrington	32	Bourne & Balmer (Croydon) Ltd
GRK	737	AEC Regal I	Harrington	32	Bourne & Balmer (Croydon) Ltd
GTF	394	Maudslay Marathon II	Longwell Green	33	Harrison and Hole
GVB	837	Crossley SD42	Whitson	33	Woodside Coaches
GVW	313	Bedford WTB	Duple	26	Classique Coaches Ltd
HGF	323	Bedford OB	Duple	32	Emerald Coaches Ltd
HGK	798	AEC Regal III	Duple	35	Eastern Belle Motor Coaches Ltd,
HLH	305	Leyland Tiger TS4	Harrington	31	Eastern Belle Motor Coaches Ltd,
HLW	981	AEC Regal I	Duple	33	Grey Green Coaches

HLW	982	AEC Regal I	Duple	33	Grey Green Coaches
HLW	983	AEC Regal I	Duple	33	Grey Green Coaches
HLW	984	AEC Regal I	Duple	33	Grey Green Coaches
HLW	985	AEC Regal I	Duple	33	Grey Green Coaches
HLW	986	AEC Regal I	Duple	33	Grey Green Coaches
HLW	987	AEC Regal I	Duple	33	Grey Green Coaches
HLX	836	Bedford OB	Duple	29	Orange Coaches (Keith & Boyle)
HMX	175	Leyland Tiger TS8	Duple	32	Henry Saloon Coaches Ltd
HMX	552	AEC Regent	(*single deck*)	32	Superior Coaches Ltd
				also	Twigg, S. V.
HMX	987	AEC Regal	Strachan	32	Wright Bros (London) Ltd
HRF	30	Leyland Tiger TS8	Willowbrook	35	McCormack, R.
HTC	283	Leyland PS1	Plaxton	32	Banfield, Charles W.
HUC	273	Leyland Lion LT5	Weymann	32	Banfield, Charles W.
HUR	621	Dennis Lancet III	Duple	35	Lee's Luxury Coaches Ltd
HUU	428	Bedford OB	Duple	27	Grey Green Coaches
HUU	429	Bedford OB	Duple	27	Grey Green Coaches
HUU	432	Bedford OB	Duple	27	Grey Green Coaches
HUU	433	Bedford OB	Duple	27	Grey Green Coaches
HUU	852	AEC Regal I	Duple	32	Bradshaw's Super Coaches Ltd
HUU	853	AEC Regal I	Duple	33	Bradshaw's Super Coaches Ltd
HUV	768	Leyland Tiger TS4	Harrington	32	Lawrence Bros (Transport) Ltd
HUW	164	Bedford OB	Duple	26	Ansell's Coaches
HVW	706	Bedford OLD	?	25	Boughton's Coaches Ltd
HXA	290	AEC Regal I	Beadle	32	Grundon, W. E.
HXA	291	AEC Regal I	Beadle	32	Grundon, W. E.
HXB	200	AEC Regal	Duple	32	Grey Coaches
HXB	457	AEC Regal I	Duple	33	Bradshaw's Super Coaches Ltd
HXB	458	AEC Regal I	Duple	33	Bradshaw's Super Coaches Ltd
HXB	459	AEC Regal I	Duple	33	Bradshaw's Super Coaches Ltd
HXB	711	Bedford OB	Duple	27	Orange Coaches (Keith & Boyle)
HXB	713	Bedford OB	Duple	27	Orange Coaches (Keith & Boyle)
HXB	714	Bedford OB	Duple	27	Orange Coaches (Keith & Boyle)
HXB	715	Bedford OB	Duple	27	Orange Coaches (Keith & Boyle)
HXB	717	Bedford OB	Duple	27	Orange Coaches (Keith & Boyle)
HXB	721	Bedford OB	Duple	27	Orange Coaches (Keith & Boyle)
HXB	723	Bedford OB	Duple	27	Orange Coaches (Keith & Boyle)
HXB	726	Bedford OB	Duple	27	Orange Coaches (Keith & Boyle)
HXB	727	Bedford OB	Duple	27	Orange Coaches (Keith & Boyle)
HXW	113	Bedford OB	Duple	29	Cliff's Saloon Coaches Ltd
HXW	746	AEC Regal	Plaxton	33	Eastern Belle Motor Coaches Ltd,
HXX	47	Maudslay Marathon II	Duple	33	Lewis, C. G.
HXX	48	Maudslay Marathon II	Duple	33	Lewis, C. G.
HXX	49	Maudslay Marathon II	Duple	33	Lewis, C. G.
HXX	50	Maudslay Marathon II	Duple	33	Lewis, C. G.
HXX	534	AEC Regal III	Beadle	32	R.A.C.S.
HXX	535	AEC Regal III	Beadle	32	R.A.C.S.
HXX	536	AEC Regal III	Beadle	32	R.A.C.S.
HXX	537	AEC Regal III	Beadle	32	R.A.C.S.
HXX	538	AEC Regal III	Beadle	32	R.A.C.S.
HXX	539	AEC Regal III	Beadle	32	R.A.C.S.
HXX	540	AEC Regal III	Duple	32	R.A.C.S.
HXX	541	AEC Regal III	Duple	32	R.A.C.S.
HXX	632	Bedford OB	Duple	29	Bradshaw's Super Coaches Ltd
HXX	828	Bedford OB	Duple	29	Cliff's Saloon Coaches Ltd
HXX	972	Bedford OB	Duple	29	Rose Transport Co. Ltd
HXY	214	Bedford OB	Duple	29	Popular Coaches Ltd
HXY	215	Bedford OB	Duple	29	Popular Coaches Ltd
HXY	508	Maudslay Marathon II	Duple	35	Ansell's Coaches
HYE	184	Commer Commando	Plaxton	30	Davis, Fred & Sons
HYE	297	Bedford OB	Duple	29	Bradshaw's Super Coaches Ltd
HYE	300	Bedford OB	Duple	29	Bradshaw's Super Coaches Ltd
HYE	762	Bedford OB	Whitson	29	Robin & Rambler Coaches Ltd
HYE	800	AEC Regal	Duple	32	Grey Coaches
HYE	927	Bedford OB	Duple	29	Sceptre Coaches
HYE	972	Leyland PS1/1	Harrington	33	Grey Green Coaches

HYF 532	Bedford OB	Duple	27	United Service Transport Co. Ltd
HYF 906	Bedford OWB	Duple	29	Camden Coaches Ltd
HYH 556	Bedford OB	Duple	27	Orange Coaches (Keith & Boyle)
HYH 557	Bedford OB	Duple	27	Orange Coaches (Keith & Boyle)
HYH 560	Bedford OB	Duple	27	Orange Coaches (Keith & Boyle)
HYH 570	Bedford OB	Duple	27	Orange Coaches (Keith & Boyle)
HYH 575	Leyland PS1/1	Harrington	33	Grey Green Coaches
HYH 576	Leyland PS1/1	Harrington	33	Grey Green Coaches
HYH 577	Leyland PS1/1	Harrington	33	Grey Green Coaches
HYH 912	Bedford OB	Duple	27	Sydenham Coaches
HYH 919	Bedford OB	Duple	27	Orange Coaches (Keith & Boyle)
HYK 235	Bedford OB	Duple	27	United Service Transport Co. Ltd
HYK 367	Morris Commercial	?	29	Camden Coaches Ltd
HYK 836	Bedford OB	Duple	29	Camden Coaches Ltd
HYK 991	Bedford OB	Duple	29	Fallowfield & Britten Ltd
HYK 992	Bedford OB	Duple	29	Fallowfield & Britten Ltd
HYK 993	Bedford OB	Duple	29	Fallowfield & Britten Ltd
			also	Empress Motors Ltd
HYM 187	AEC Regal I	Harrington	32	Bradshaw's Super Coaches Ltd
HYM 329	Maudslay Marathon III	Whitson	33	Progress Coaches
HYM 685	Bedford OB	Duple	29	Fallowfield & Britten Ltd
HYN 420	Bedford OB	Duple	29	Bradshaw's Super Coaches Ltd
HYN 461	Bedford OB	Duple	29	Hall's Coaches
HYN 462	Leyland PS1/1	Duple	35	Ferndale Coaches
HYN 466	Leyland PS1	Harrington	33	Argosy Super Coaches
HYN 467	Bedford OB	Duple	29	Banfield, Charles W.
HYN 479	Bedford OB	Duple	29	Fallowfield & Britten Ltd
HYN 480	Bedford OB	Duple	29	Fallowfield & Britten Ltd
HYN 488	AEC Regal	Duple	35	Clarke's Luxury Coaches
HYN 490	Dennis Lancet III	Duple	35	Clarke's Luxury Coaches
HYN 566	Commer Commando	Strachan	20	Red Line Continental Motorways
HYN 688	Bedford OB	Duple	29	Cliff's Saloon Coaches Ltd
HYN 699	Bedford OB	Duple	29	Down, A. P.
HYN 700	Bedford OB	Duple	29	Sceptre Coaches
HYO 97	Bedford OB	Duple	29	Pritchard, John
HYO 197	Bedford OB	Duple	27	Frame's Tours Ltd
HYO 260	Leyland PS1/1	Strachan	33	United Service Transport Co. Ltd
HYO 261	Leyland PS1/1	Strachan	33	United Service Transport Co. Ltd
HYO 262	Leyland PS1/1	Strachan	33	United Service Transport Co. Ltd
HYO 300	AEC Regal I	Harrington	32	Bradshaw's Super Coaches Ltd
HYO 356	Maudslay Marathon III	Whitson	33	Robin & Rambler Coaches Ltd
HYO 357	Maudslay Marathon III	Whitson	33	Robin & Rambler Coaches Ltd
HYO 495	Bedford OB	Duple	29	Fallowfield & Britten Ltd
HYO 690	Bedford OB	Duple	29	Grey Green Coaches
HYO 705	Dennis Lancet III	Duple	35	Empress Motors Ltd
HYO 706	Bedford OB	Duple	29	Empress Motors Ltd
HYO 981	Bedford OB	Duple	29	Bradshaw's Super Coaches Ltd
HYO 985	Bedford OB	Duple	29	Bradshaw's Super Coaches Ltd
HYO 988	Bedford OB	Duple	29	Bradshaw's Super Coaches Ltd
HYO 990	Bedford OB	Duple	29	Cliff's Saloon Coaches Ltd
HYP 210	Bedford OB	Duple	27	United Service Transport Co. Ltd
HYP 220	Dennis Lancet III	Duple	35	Emerald Coaches Ltd
HYP 328	Leyland PS1/1	Strachan	33	United Service Transport Co. Ltd
HYP 329	Leyland PS1/1	Strachan	33	United Service Transport Co. Ltd
HYP 330	Leyland PS1/1	Strachan	33	United Service Transport Co. Ltd
HYP 559	Bedford OB	Duple	29	Empress Motors Ltd
			also	Fallowfield & Britten Ltd
HYP 560	Bedford OB	Duple	29	Grey Green Coaches
HYP 775	Bedford OB	Duple	29	Grove Coaches
HYP 847	Bedford OB	Duple	27	Frame's Tours Ltd
HYP 901	Bedford OB	Duple	29	Grey Green Coaches
HYR 192	Leyland PS1/1	Strachan	33	United Service Transport Co. Ltd
HYR 193	Leyland PS1/1	Strachan	33	United Service Transport Co. Ltd
HYR 194	Leyland PS1/1	Strachan	33	United Service Transport Co. Ltd
HYR 257	Bedford OB	Duple	29	Camden Coaches Ltd
HYR 440	Leyland PS1/1	Strachan	33	United Service Transport Co. Ltd

HYR	586	Leyland PS1/1	Strachan	33	United Service Transport Co. Ltd
HYR	782	Leyland PS1/1	Duple	33	United Service Transport Co. Ltd
HYR	783	Leyland PS1/1	Duple	33	United Service Transport Co. Ltd
HYU	82	Maudslay Marathon III	Whitson	33	Majestic Luxury Coaches Ltd
HYU	539	Leyland PS1/1	Strachan	25	Red Line Continental Motorways
HYU	786	Bedford OB	Duple	29	Empress Motors Ltd
JAE	332	Bedford OWB	Duple	28	Tyler, R. A.
JAL	82	Commer Q4	Plaxton	30	Radio Coaches
JAR	954	Bedford OB	Thurgood	29	Premier Omnibus Company
JGY	448	AEC Regal III	Strachan	32	Red Line Continental Motorways
JKN	885	Dennis Lancet	?	31	Gilbert's Luxury Coaches Ltd
JLG	991	Bedford OB	Plaxton	29	Holder, A. R. & Sons Ltd
JLH	237	Leyland PS1/1	Duple	35	Grey Green Coaches
JLH	238	Leyland PS1/1	Duple	35	Grey Green Coaches
JLH	239	Leyland PS1/1	Duple	35	Grey Green Coaches
JLH	240	Leyland PS1/1	Duple	35	Grey Green Coaches
JLH	241	Leyland PS1/1	Duple	35	Grey Green Coaches
JLM	501	AEC Regal	Harrington	33	Bradshaw's Super Coaches Ltd
JMC	271	Albion Valkyrie CX9	Mulliner	33	A and W Omnibus Co. Ltd
JMC	987	AEC Regal I	Duple	32	Lily Coaches
JMC	994	Dennis Lancet II	Duple	35	Garner's Coaches Ltd
JNK	500	Dennis Lancet III	Duple	35	Gatehouse Coaches
JPK	498	Bedford OWB	Duple	32	Blue & White Star Transport Co. Ltd
JPK	871	Bedford OWB	Duple	32	Blue & White Star Transport Co. Ltd
JPK	872	Bedford OWB	Duple	32	Blue & White Star Transport Co. Ltd
JPL	163	Bedford OWB	Duple	32	Stanley, Ben Ltd
JTE	704	Leyland PS1/1	Burlingham	33	Lacey's (East Ham) Ltd
JTW	333	Bedford OWB	Duple	32	Leighton Coach Co. Ltd
JTW	334	Bedford OWB	Duple	26	Leighton Coach Co. Ltd
JTW	335	Bedford OWB	Duple	28	Leighton Coach Co. Ltd
JUV	297	Bedford OB	Duple	29	Bradshaw's Super Coaches Ltd
JUV	352	Dennis Lancet III	Duple	33	Empress Coaches
JXB	23	Maudslay Marathon III	Whitson	33	Majestic Luxury Coaches Ltd
JXB	321	Bedford OB	Whitson	29	Robin & Rambler Coaches Ltd
JXB	322	Bedford OB	Whitson	29	Robin & Rambler Coaches Ltd
JXC	778	Dennis Lancet III	Duple	35	Clarke's Luxury Coaches
JXC	780	Dennis Lancet III	Duple	33	Monico Motorways
JXD	214	Maudslay Marathon III	Whitson	33	Majestic Luxury Coaches Ltd
JXD	650	Bedford OB	Duple	29	Clarke's Luxury Coaches
JXD	750	Bedford OB	Mulliner	28	Lawrence Bros (Transport) Ltd
JXE	296	Maudslay Marathon III	Westnor	33	Ubique Coaches
JXE	956	Bedford OB	Whitson	29	Robin & Rambler Coaches Ltd
JXF	327	Bedford OB	Duple	29	Empress Motors Ltd
JXH	163	Bedford OB	Duple	29	Banfield, Charles W.
JXH	169	Commer Commando	Allweather	30	J. M. Motors
JXH	515	Leyland PS1/1	Duple	33	Lewis, C. G.
JXH	545	Bedford OB	Duple	29	Cliff's Saloon Coaches Ltd
JXH	555	Bedford OB	Duple	29	Carshalton & Wallington Coaches
JXH	768	AEC Regal	Plaxton	33	Eastern Belle Motor Coaches Ltd,
JXK	884	Commer	?	32	Mountain Transport Services Ltd
JXL	60	Bedford OB	Duple	29	Futcher, G. J.
JXL	376	Bedford OB	Duple	29	Empress Motors Ltd
JXL	377	Dennis Lancet III	Duple	35	Empress Motors Ltd
JXL	451	Leyland PS1	Strachan	32	Banfield, Charles W.
JXL	452	Leyland PS1	Strachan	32	Banfield, Charles W.
JXL	478	Bedford OB	Duple	29	Banfield, Charles W.
JXL	558	Bedford OB	Duple	29	Manny, L. Ltd
JXM	763	Daimler CVD6	Harrington	33	Bradshaw's Super Coaches Ltd
JXN	626	Commer Commando	Allweather	30	J. M. Motors
JXP	100	Tilling Stevens K6LA7	Dutfield	33	Grey Coaches
JXP	453	Bedford OB	Duple	29	Cliff's Saloon Coaches Ltd
JXP	488	Dennis Lancet III	Whitson	35	R.A.C.S.
JXT	527	AEC Regal III	Duple	33	Clarke's Luxury Coaches
JXT	614	Bedford OB	Woodall Nicholson	29	Dryer's Coaches Ltd
JXT	615	Bedford OB	Woodall Nicholson	29	Rose Transport Co. Ltd
JXT	788	Austin CXB	Plaxton	29	Grove Coaches

KGH	310	Bedford OB	Duple	29	Camden Coaches Ltd
KGN	924	Bedford OB	Plaxton	30	Boughton's Coaches Ltd
KGT	17	Maudslay Marathon III	Duple	32	Harrison and Hole
KGT	18	Dennis Lancet III	Duple	35	Clarke's Luxury Coaches
KGT	424	Bedford OB	Plaxton	30	Boughton's Coaches Ltd
KGT	598	Commer Commando	Pearson	30	Lawrence Bros (Transport) Ltd
KGT	977	Crossley SD42/7	Santus	33	Mountain Transport Services Ltd
KGW	20	Austin CXB	Mann Egerton	31	Mountain Transport Services Ltd
KGW	566	Commer Commando	Allweather	30	J. M. Motors
KLM	150	Austin CXB	Mann Egerton	29	Hampton Coaches
KMG	450	Bedford WTB	Thurgood	26	Modern Super Coaches
KPA	139	Leyland Tiger TS7	Harrington	32	United Service Transport Co. Ltd
KPA	271	Bedford OWB	Duple	32	Graves, G. F. & Son
KPA	298	Bedford OWB	Duple	32	Stanley, Ben Ltd
KPB	265	Bedford OWB	Duple	27	Stanley, Ben Ltd
KPG	997	AEC Regal	Duple	32	Davis, L. C. & Sons
KPU	851	AEC Regal	King & Taylor	32	Gidea Park Coaches Ltd
KPU	852	AEC Regal	King & Taylor	32	Gidea Park Coaches Ltd
KPU	854	AEC Regal	King & Taylor	32	Gidea Park Coaches Ltd
KRF	106	Bedford OWB	Mulliner	28	Castle Coaches
KRF	111	Bedford OWB	Mulliner	28	Castle Coaches
KRF	114	Bedford OWB	Mulliner	29	Castle Coaches
KRF	853	Dennis Lancet	?	38	Barking Coaches Ltd
KYC	326	Crossley SD42/3	Windover	33	Clarke's Luxury Coaches
KYC	327	Crossley SD42/3	Windover	33	Clarke's Luxury Coaches
LHK	913	Maudslay Marathon II	Duple	33	Classique Coaches Ltd
LME	665	Leyland Tiger TS7	Duple	33	Henry Saloon Coaches Ltd
LME	673	AEC Regal	Duple	33	Ferndale Coaches
LMG	475	Bedford OWB	Duple	28	Elms, Phillips & Brown
LMG	484	Bedford OWB	Duple	28	Carshalton & Wallington Coaches
LMG	526	Leyland Tiger TS8	Duple	32	Valliant Direct Motor Coaches Ltd
LMG	629	Bedford OB	Duple	32	Horseshoe Coaches
LMG	650	Bedford OB	Duple	32	White Line Coaches
LMH	955	Leyland Tiger TS4	Duple	32	Broadway Coaches
LML	154	Bedford OWB	Mulliner	32	Universal Coaches Ltd
LML	157	Bedford OWB	Duple	32	Davis, L. C. & Sons
LML	486	Bedford OWB	Duple	32	Universal Coaches Ltd
LML	513	Bedford OWB	Duple	28	Winfield's Coaches
LMT	82	Leyland Tiger TS4	Duple	32	Valliant Direct Motor Coaches Ltd
LMT	602	Bedford	?	?	Universal Coaches Ltd
LMT	613	Bedford OWB	Duple	32	Davis, L. C. & Sons
LMT	704	Bedford OWB	Duple	32	A and W Omnibus Co. Ltd
LMT	880	Bedford OWB	Duple	32	Grosvenor Coaches Ltd
LMV	387	AEC Regal	Duple	32	Davis, L. C. & Sons
LMX	111	Dennis Lancet	Dennis	32	Acorn Motors Ltd
LMY	254	Bedford OB	Duple	27	Garner's Coaches Ltd
LMY	260	AEC Regal	Park Royal	32	Superior Coaches Ltd
LMY	449	Bedford OB	Duple	29	Essex County Coaches
LMY	450	Bedford OB	Duple	29	Essex County Coaches
LMY	462	Bedford OB	Duple	27	Garner's Coaches Ltd
LMY	645	Dennis Lancet	?	34	Acorn Motors Ltd
LMY	646	Bedford WTB	?	25	Acorn Motors Ltd
LMY	682	Bedford OB	Duple	29	Essex County Coaches
LMY	893	Bedford OB	Duple	29	Hall's Coaches
LNO	91	Maudslay Marathon II	Duple	33	Classique Coaches Ltd
LNO	298	Maudslay Marathon II	Duple	33	Classique Coaches Ltd
LNO	299	Maudslay Marathon II	Duple	33	Classique Coaches Ltd
LNO	414	Albion PW67	Cowieson ?	32	Dagenham Coach Services
LPB	4	Bedford OB	Duple	29	Graves, G. F. & Son
LPB	748	Bedford OB	Whitson	27	Majestic Luxury Coaches Ltd
LPB	749	Maudslay Marathon III	Whitson	33	Green Luxury Coaches
LPB	750	Maudslay Marathon III	Whitson	33	Green Luxury Coaches
LPC	851	Bedford OB	Duple	27	United Service Transport Co. Ltd
LPE	123	Bedford OB	Duple	28	Graves, G. F. & Son
LPF	249	Bedford OB	Whitson	27	Majestic Luxury Coaches Ltd
LPF	876	AEC Regal	Dutfield	32	Davis, L. C. & Sons

LPH	429	Maudslay Marathon III	Whitson	32	Green Luxury Coaches
LPJ	129	Maudslay Marathon III	Whitson	32	Green Luxury Coaches
LPL	800	AEC Regal	King & Taylor	33	Davis, L. C. & Sons
LTW	461	Bedford OB	Duple	29	Leighton Coach Co. Ltd
LVX	467	Maudslay Marathon II	Whitson	33	Pathfinder Luxury Coaches
LVX	468	Maudslay Marathon III	Whitson	33	Pathfinder Luxury Coaches
MEV	321	Bedford OB	Black & White	28	Black & White Coaches Ltd
MEV	391	Maudslay Marathon II	Whitson	33	Pathfinder Luxury Coaches
MEV	799	Maudslay Marathon II	Westnor	33	Majestic Luxury Coaches Ltd
MHK	548	Guy Arab III	Strachan	33	Dix Luxury Coaches
MHK	549	Guy Arab III	Strachan	33	Dix Luxury Coaches
MHX	321	AEC Regal	Strachan	35	Wright Bros (London) Ltd
MME	45	AEC Regent	Burlingham (*sing. deck*)	32	Superior Coaches Ltd
MME	153	Leyland Tiger TS4	Harrington	32	Henry Saloon Coaches Ltd
MME	154	Leyland Tiger TS8	Harrington	32	Henry Saloon Coaches Ltd
MME	364	Commer Commando	Strachan	32	Wright Bros (London) Ltd
MME	742	Bedford OB	Duple	29	Davis, L. C. & Sons
MME	743	Bedford OB	Duple	29	Davis, L. C. & Sons
MME	744	Bedford OB	Duple	29	Davis, L. C. & Sons
MME	745	Bedford OB	Duple	29	Davis, L. C. & Sons
MMH	234	Commer Commando	Strachan	32	Wright Bros (London) Ltd
MMH	618	Bedford OB	Duple	27	United Service Transport Co. Ltd
MMH	619	Bedford OB	Duple	27	United Service Transport Co. Ltd
MML	496	Bedford OB	Duple	29	Thorne Bros.
MMP	169	Bedford OB	Duple	29	Crouch End Luxury
MMP	170	Bedford OB	Duple	29	Crouch End Luxury
MMP	171	AEC Regal	Duple	35	Crouch End Luxury
MMP	578	Bedford OB	Duple	29	Winwood Coaches Ltd
MMP	579	Bedford OB	Duple	29	Winwood Coaches Ltd
MMP	813	Bedford OB	Duple	29	Essex County Coaches
MMP	815	Bedford OB	Duple	29	Valliant Direct Motor Coaches Ltd
MMT	506	Bedford OB	Duple	29	Garner's Coaches Ltd
MMT	507	Bedford OB	Duple	29	Garner's Coaches Ltd
MMT	508	Bedford OB	Duple	29	Garner's Coaches Ltd
MMT	861	Bedford OB	Duple	27	Garner's Coaches Ltd
MMT	862	Bedford OB	Duple	27	Garner's Coaches Ltd
MMT	863	Bedford OB	Duple	27	Garner's Coaches Ltd
MMT	864	Bedford OB	Duple	27	Garner's Coaches Ltd
MMT	865	Bedford OB	Duple	27	Garner's Coaches Ltd
MMT	866	Bedford OB	Duple	27	Garner's Coaches Ltd
MMT	875	Bedford OB	Duple	29	Fallowfield & Britten Ltd
MMT	877	Bedford OB	Duple	29	Fallowfield & Britten Ltd
MMT	879	Bedford OB	Duple	29	Ray (Edgware) Ltd
MMT	880	Bedford OB	Duple	27	Ray (Edgware) Ltd
MMY	104	AEC Regal I	Duple	33	Lily Coaches
MMY	105	AEC Regal I	Duple	33	Lily Coaches
MMY	114	AEC Regal	Strachan	35	Wright Bros (London) Ltd
MMY	370	AEC Regal	Strachan	35	Wright Bros (London) Ltd
MMY	454	AEC Regal	Strachan	32	Valliant Direct Motor Coaches Ltd
MMY	680	Bedford OB	Duple	27	Empress Coaches
MMY	696	Bedford OB	Duple	29	Hall Brothers
MNO	144	Maudslay Marathon III	Whitson	33	Pathfinder Luxury Coaches
MPA	686	Maudslay Marathon III	Dutfield	33	A and W Omnibus Co. Ltd
MPA	688	Maudslay Marathon	Dutfield	33	A and W Omnibus Co. Ltd
MPA	689	Maudslay Marathon III	Dutfield	33	Grundon, W. E.
MPA	690	Maudslay Marathon III	Dutfield	33	Grundon, W. E.
MPB	333	Bedford OB	Duple	29	Hall's Coaches
MPB	891	Maudslay Marathon	Dutfield	33	A and W Omnibus Co. Ltd
MPB	894	Crossley SD42	Dutfield	33	Elms, Longman Motor Services Ltd
MPU	61	Bedford OB	Black & White	29	Emerald Coaches Ltd
MPU	62	Bedford OB	Black & White	29	Emerald Coaches Ltd
MPU	348	Bedford OB	Duple	29	Thorpe Coaches Ltd
MPU	400	Maudslay Marathon II	Duple	35	Classique Coaches Ltd
MTW	985	Maudslay Marathon II	Whitson	33	Universal Coaches Ltd
				also	Dix Luxury Coaches
MVW	15	Maudslay Marathon II	Whitson	33	Champion Coaches

MVW 155	Bedford OB	Duple	29	Dryer's Coaches Ltd
MVW 725	Austin CXB	Mann Egerton	29	Dix Luxury Coaches
MVX 376	Bedford OB	Duple	29	Dix Luxury Coaches
MVX 881	Maudslay Marathon II	Whitson	35	Universal Coaches Ltd
			also	Dix Luxury Coaches
NEV 190	Bedford OB	Whitson	29	Dix Luxury Coaches
NHK 984	AEC Regal 3	Plaxton	33	Green, A. & Sons
NNO 111	AEC Regal 3	Plaxton	33	Green, A. & Sons
NNO 229	Bedford OB	Strachan	29	Dix Luxury Coaches
NPU 424	Bedford OB	Duple	29	Safeway Coaches
NRF 301	Bedford OB	Burlingham	26	Emerald Coaches Ltd
NTW 86	Leyland Cub SKP	?	20	Twigg, S. V.
NTW 140	Crossley SD4?/7	Whitson	33	Champion Coaches
NTW 222	Maudslay Marathon III	Whitson	33	Green, A. & Sons
NTW 706	Bedford OB	Duple	29	Dix Luxury Coaches
NVW 11	Maudslay Marathon III	Santus	33	Green, A. & Sons
OML 97	Commer Commando	Harrington	30	Lucky Line Coaches Ltd
OML 293	AEC Regal	Strachan	33	Valliant Direct Motor Coaches Ltd
OML 294	AEC Regal	Strachan	33	Valliant Direct Motor Coaches Ltd
OML 312	Bedford OB	Duple	29	Elms, Phillips & Brown
OML 459	AEC Regal	Bush & Twiddy	32	Superior Coaches Ltd
OML 605	Leyland PS1/1	Duple	35	Henry Saloon Coaches Ltd
OML 825	Bedford OB	Duple	29	Cronshaw, Lewis Ltd
OML 915	Bedford OB	Duple	28	Criterion Coaches Ltd
OMT 80	Leyland Tiger TS7	Burlingham	32	Valliant Direct Motor Coaches Ltd
OMT 367	Maudslay Marathon III	Strachan	33	Enterprise Coaches
OMT 373	Leyland PS1/1	Duple	33	Venture Transport (Hendon) Ltd
OMT 409	Maudslay Marathon III	Whitson	33	A and W Omnibus Co. Ltd
OMT 410	Maudslay Marathon III	Whitson	33	A and W Omnibus Co. Ltd
OMT 411	Maudslay Marathon III	Whitson	33	A and W Omnibus Co. Ltd
OMT 412	Maudslay Marathon III	Whitson	33	A and W Omnibus Co. Ltd
OMT 456	Leyland Tiger TS6	?	32	Valliant Direct Motor Coaches Ltd
OMT 555	Leyland Tiger TS7	Valliant	32	Valliant Direct Motor Coaches Ltd
OMT 602	Bedford OB	Duple	29	Ardley Brothers Ltd
OMY 378	Bedford OB	Duple	29	Elms, Phillips & Brown
OMY 385	Bedford OB	Duple	29	Garner's Coaches Ltd
OMY 386	Bedford OB	Duple	29	Garner's Coaches Ltd
OMY 405	AEC Regal I	Duple	35	Lily Coaches
OMY 410	Bedford OB	Duple	29	Ardley Brothers Ltd
OMY 449	Dennis Lancet	Duple	35	Horseshoe Coaches
OMY 465	Maudslay Marathon	Whitson	33	A and W Omnibus Co. Ltd
OMY 502	AEC Regal	Whitson	35	Wright Bros (London) Ltd
OMY 520	Bedford OB	Duple	29	Ardley Brothers Ltd
OMY 533	Maudslay Marathon III	Whitson	35	Wright Bros (London) Ltd
OMY 583	Maudslay Marathon III	Whitson	33	A and W Omnibus Co. Ltd
OMY 584	Maudslay Marathon III	Whitson	33	A and W Omnibus Co. Ltd
OMY 585	Maudslay Marathon	Whitson	33	A and W Omnibus Co. Ltd
ORE 651	Leyland Tiger TS1	E.C.O.C.	29	Wayfarer Coaches
SME 9	Bedford OB	Whitson	27	Wright Bros (London) Ltd
SME 12	Maudslay Marathon III	Whitson	33	Valliant Direct Motor Coaches Ltd
SME 81	AEC Regal I	Brush	33	Venture Transport (Hendon) Ltd
SME 82	AEC Regal I	Brush	33	Venture Transport (Hendon) Ltd
SME 83	AEC Regal I	Brush	33	Venture Transport (Hendon) Ltd
SME 84	AEC Regal I	Brush	33	Venture Transport (Hendon) Ltd
SME 229	AEC Regal I	Duple	35	Lily Coaches
SME 230	AEC Regal I	?	35	Lily Coaches
SME 291	Commer Commando	Whitson	31	Wright Bros (London) Ltd
SME 292	Commer Commando	Whitson	31	Wright Bros (London) Ltd
SME 293	Commer Commando	Whitson	31	Wright Bros (London) Ltd
SME 314	Dennis Lancet III	Duple	35	Garner's Coaches Ltd
SME 323	Leyland Lion LT7	?	34	Valliant Direct Motor Coaches Ltd
SMF 8	Bedford OB	Duple	27	Ardley Brothers Ltd
SMF 316	Commer Commando	Strachan	31	Wright Bros (London) Ltd
SMF 317	Commer Commando	Strachan	31	Wright Bros (London) Ltd
SMF 338	Maudslay Marathon III	Whitson	33	A and W Omnibus Co. Ltd
SMF 339	Maudslay Marathon III	Westnor	33	A and W Omnibus Co. Ltd

SMF	380	Bedford OB	Thurgood	29	Horseshoe Coaches
SMF	530	Bedford OB	Duple	29	Viney's Luxury Coaches
SMF	585	Bedford OB	Duple	27	Ardley Brothers Ltd
SMF	605	Bedford OB	Duple	29	Valliant Direct Motor Coaches Ltd
SMF	632	Bedford OB	Duple	29	Thorne Bros.
SMF	946	Leyland PS1/1	Duple	35	Henry Saloon Coaches Ltd
SMF	961	Bedford OB	Duple	29	Modern Super Coaches
SML	10	AEC Regal III	Duple	33	Lily Coaches
SML	50	Maudslay Marathon III	Whitson	35	Valliant Direct Motor Coaches Ltd
SML	139	AEC Regal	?	32	Superior Coaches Ltd
SML	199	Maudslay Marathon III	Whitson	33	Wright Bros (London) Ltd
SML	276	Bedford OB	Thurgood	29	Modern Super Coaches
SML	399	Leyland PS1/1	Strachan	33	Valliant Direct Motor Coaches Ltd
SML	400	Bedford OB	Duple	29	Ferndale Coaches
SML	467	Bedford OB	Duple	29	Barking Coaches Ltd
				also	Lacey's (East Ham) Ltd
SML	474	Daimler CVD6	Yorkshire Yachtbuilders	33	Emerald Coaches Ltd
SML	475	Daimler CVD6	Yorkshire Yachtbuilders	33	Emerald Coaches Ltd
SML	597	Leyland PS1/1	Duple	33	Lewis, C. G.
SML	696	Bedford OB	Duple	29	Ray (Edgware) Ltd
SMY	22	Commer Commando	Harrington	30	Lucky Line Coaches Ltd
SMY	152	Bedford OB	Duple	29	Golden Miller Coaches
SMY	248	AEC Regal III	Duple	35	Crouch End Luxury
SMY	253	AEC Regal III	Strachan	35	Wright Bros (London) Ltd
SMY	256	Bedford OB	Whitson	29	Wright Bros (London) Ltd
SMY	257	Bedford OB	Whitson	29	Wright Bros (London) Ltd
SMY	262	Bedford OB	Duple	29	Lily Coaches
SMY	294	Bedford OB	Duple	29	Lucky Line Coaches Ltd
SMY	864	Bedford OB	Duple	29	Hall's Coaches
SMY	920	Bedford OB	Duple	29	Thorne Bros.
TMG	167	Bedford OB	Strachan	29	Wright Bros (London) Ltd
TMG	168	Bedford OB	Strachan	29	Wright Bros (London) Ltd
TMG	198	Maudslay Marathon III	Whitson	35	Wright Bros (London) Ltd
TMG	687	AEC Regent	Barnaby (*single deck*)	33	Superior Coaches Ltd
TMG	688	AEC Regent	Barnaby (*single deck*)	33	Superior Coaches Ltd
TMG	690	AEC Regal	Churchill	35	Superior Coaches Ltd
TMG	691	AEC Regal	Churchill	35	Superior Coaches Ltd
TMG	724	Leyland PS1/1	Dutfield	33	Davis, L. C. & Sons
TMG	732	Bedford OB	Duple	29	Viney's Luxury Coaches
TMG	847	Daimler CVD6	Thurgood	35	Viney's Luxury Coaches
TMK	74	AEC Regal I	Strachan	35	Margo's
TMK	640	Bedford OB	Duple	29	Lacey's (East Ham) Ltd
TMV	8	Bedford OB	Duple	29	Curtis & Hearn
TMV	18	Austin CXB	Allweather	29	Cosy Coaches
TMV	115	Maudslay Marathon III	Whitson	33	A and W Omnibus Co. Ltd
TMV	116	Maudslay Marathon III	Whitson	33	A and W Omnibus Co. Ltd
TMV	262	Maudslay Marathon III	Whitson	33	A and W Omnibus Co. Ltd
TMV	311	Maudslay Marathon III	Whitson	33	A and W Omnibus Co. Ltd
TMV	502	Bedford OB	Duple	29	Banfield, Charles W.
TMV	503	Bedford OB	Duple	29	Pritchard, John
TMV	994	Leyland PS1/1	Duple	33	Davis, L. C. & Sons
TMY	677	Crossley SD42/7	Strachan	33	Viney's Luxury Coaches
TMY	717	Bedford OB	Duple	29	Gilbert's Luxury Coaches Ltd
VML	2	Bedford OB	Duple	29	Wright Bros (London) Ltd